ISSUES IN THE
DIGITAL AGE

Issues in the Digital Age

Online Communication and Social Networking

Jim Whiting

ReferencePoint Press®

San Diego, CA

© 2012 ReferencePoint Press, Inc.
Printed in the United States

For more information, contact:
ReferencePoint Press, Inc.
PO Box 27779
San Diego, CA 92198
www. ReferencePointPress.com

LIBRARY OF CONGRESS CATALOGING-IN-PUBLICATION DATA

Whiting, Jim, 1943–
Online communication and social networking / by Jim Whiting.
   p. cm. — (Issues in the digital age series)
Includes bibliographical references and index.
ISBN-13: 978-1-60152-190-3 (hbk.)
ISBN-10: 1-60152-190-1 (hbk.)
1. Online social networks—Juvenile literature. 2. Social media—Juvenile literature. 3. Digital communication—Juvenile literature. 4. Communication—Social aspects—Juvenile literature. I. Title.
 HM742.W54 2012
 303.48'33—dc23

                                          2011023648

Contents

Tweeting Oscar's Big Night

For many people, the best parts of the 2011 Oscars telecast came *after* each announcement of the award winners. In virtually every case, the winner had been predicted far in advance. Viewers had to find excitement elsewhere.

To create more excitement, the Academy of Motion Picture Arts and Sciences had selected two young hosts, Anne Hathaway and James Franco, but what made this show different from all others were the hundreds of thousands (some say millions) of Tweets on the microblogging Twitter network during the evening.

Some Tweets came from Franco himself, who, according to some critics, seemed more interested in Tweeting while he was offstage than in performing his onstage hosting duties. His mother and grandmother also participated, as the ABC network asked several mothers of nominees—Franco was up for Best Actor in addition to serving as cohost—to serve as "mominees" and Twitter during the show.

A Great Deal of Tweeting

Some Tweeting involved putdowns of the proceedings. "I'm only watching the Oscars so I can Tweet about it with everyone,"[1] said one person. Many Tweets, however, seemed to show a genuine interest. Best Supporting Actress winner Melissa Leo generated nearly 11,000 Tweets early in the broadcast when she dropped the first-ever f-bomb at the Oscars. Later, Oprah Winfrey reached the maximum rate of 11,780 Tweets a minute when she announced the winner of the Best Documentary Feature.

Twitter did not provide the only social networking that evening. When they were not Tweeting, many viewers were on Facebook. Nearly 2 million Facebook status updates were connected to the broadcast. ABC also set up a site called Oscars.com to provide a behind-the-scenes look at the evening's events. It included live video streams of the winners as soon as they went backstage.

Twitter, Facebook, Oscars.com, and their like represent a significant shift in the way that people watch the show. In previous years people sat passively, perhaps getting up during commercial breaks but otherwise rooted to their couches and sharing their opinions with the few people watching along with them. But this time huge numbers of viewers became actively involved during the telecast and found a far larger audience for their thoughts.

The Tweeting public was the real star of the 2011 Academy Awards, cohosted by actors Anne Hathaway and James Franco (pictured). Franco fit right in with this new reality, Tweeting throughout the show even while on stage.

This active involvement in the Oscars is just one of a countless number of examples of how social networking and online communication have revolutionized people's lives. They have become integral elements of daily life for hundreds of millions of people around the world, in ways unforeseen even a decade ago. The social aspect is apparent as many people spend hours every day keeping up with what their online friends are doing and, in turn, heralding their own accomplishments.

A New Way of Life

Social media pervade many other areas as well. In 2011 basketball star Shaquille O'Neal announced his retirement on Twitter. More than 700 wives of college sports coaches belong to MarriedToTheGame.net, an online site that provides a venue for the women to bond with others who have similar experiences. Millions of businesspeople use sites such as Linked-In to broaden their professional affiliations. From the far right to the far left, advocacy groups find the Internet a persuasive—and inexpensive—means of getting their message across.

Many Republicans felt that President Obama's ease and familiarity with social media was a major contributor to his victory in the 2008 presidential election, and they moved quickly to end that advantage in the 2010 mid-term elections. "You learn more from losing than winning sometimes," says Matt Lira, director of new media for House Republican majority leader Eric Cantor. "You did not become a top recruit for the House unless you intended to make a robust use of the Web."[2]

> "I'm only watching the Oscars so I can Tweet about it with everyone."[1]
>
> — A 2011 Academy Awards viewer.

And at the same time that Franco and Hathaway opened the Oscar telecast, tens of thousands of Egyptians, organized and encouraged by sites such as Facebook and Twitter, filled the streets of their capital city of Cairo. Social media offered them a way to protest after years of passively accepting the rule of an often brutal regime.

In this sense, therefore, the two favorites for the coveted Best Picture Oscar served as symbolic bookends for the rise in importance of social media. *The King's Speech*, the winner, is set at the beginning of the age of modern mass communication. *The Social Network* focuses on Facebook, which in just a few years following its founding has become the most far-reaching and influential form of social networking.

In short, social media have become an all-pervasive, all-encompassing fact of modern life. From dating sites to data searches, from friends to "frenemies," from OMG to online movie guides, there are few aspects of contemporary society that have not felt its impact. And these revolution-ary changes have occurred in less than two decades.

Chapter One

The Wired World

Sohaib Athar was annoyed. The 33-year-old Pakistani was sitting at his computer after midnight on May 2, 2011, when a loud clattering disturbed his concentration. Getting away from commotion was a primary reason he and his family had moved from the teeming city of Lahore to the much smaller town of Abbottabad, tucked away in the mountains in the northern part of the country. For several months, Athar had reveled in the quiet of a town that was home to many lawyers, doctors, retired military officers, and other well-to-do Pakistanis. *Time* magazine's Aryn Baker describes Abbottabad as a place where "colonial-era bungalows abut modern whitewashed villas on small streets largely devoid of traffic. It's the kind of place where families take a stroll as the day cools into night, where you might still go and ask a neighbor for a cup of sugar."[3]

Despite Abbottabad's remoteness, Athar, a coffee-shop owner and information technology consultant, was a frequent and enthusiastic participant in social networking and online communication. As the disturbance continued, he sent a Tweet to his 750 or so followers: "Helicopter hovering above Abbottabad at 1AM (is a rare event)." Seven minutes later, he sent another: "Go away helicopter—before I take out my giant swatter:-/" Within four minutes, things really started hopping: "A huge window shaking bang here in Abbottabad Cantt. I hope its not the start of something nasty:-S"[4]

"Something nasty" was indeed starting in Abbottabad. After months of painstaking investigation, President Barack Obama had concluded that Osama bin Laden, the architect of the 9/11 attacks and almost certainly the most hated man in the United States, was living there. The clattering of the helicopters marked the beginning of the raid that would result in his death.

The World Becomes Aware

Athar's Tweets were the first outside evidence of the raid, which had been planned and launched under the strictest secrecy. He continued Tweeting through the night, reporting rumors and bits of information from his neighbors, though he still had no idea of what was going on. Thanks at least in part to his Tweeting, more and more people around the world began to suspect the truth. They were not hesitant about sharing the news, whether through Twitter, Facebook, e-mail alerts from major newspapers or other nontraditional forms of communication. One of the most definitive Tweets came at 10:24 p.m. eastern daylight time from Keith Urbahn, chief of staff for former defense secretary Donald Rumsfeld: "So I'm told by a reputable person they have killed Osama Bin Laden. Hot damn."[5]

The first public account of the US raid on Osama bin Laden's compound in Pakistan came not from a major newspaper or even from the government but from an unsuspecting neighbor Tweeting about the strange goings-on in the middle of the night. Only later did he learn the reason for the nighttime disturbance.

So by the time that President Obama began speaking on national television shortly after 11:30 that night, his announcement of Bin Laden's death simply confirmed what many people felt they already knew. Americans in untold numbers poured out into the streets in impromptu celebrations, many of which were captured by camera phones and posted on YouTube and Facebook. The news also resulted in at least 5 million Facebook status updates and a flood of Tweets, one of which noted the near overlap of the British royal wedding and the raid: "A prince gets married, the bad guy is dead. It's a real Disney weekend here on earth."[6] The entire phenomenon caused Chris Cillizza of the political website The Fix, to say (in a Tweet, of course), "If anyone isn't a believer in Twitter as an amazingly powerful news vehicle, last night should convert you."[7]

> **"I'm the guy who liveblogged the Osama raid without knowing it."**[9]
>
> —Sohaib Athar, Pakistani Tweeter.

Soon after Obama's announcement—mid-morning the following day in Abbottabad—the online communication of the night before came full circle. Athar Tweeted: "Osama Bin Laden killed in Abbottabad, Pakistan. . . .There goes the neighborhood."[8] By then he had nearly 100,000 followers and a reputation as "I'm the guy who liveblogged the Osama raid without knowing it."[9]

Preserving Precious Memories

A few days before the raid, Facebook revealed a different aspect of the immense power of social media in reacting to death and destruction. The devastating tornadoes that killed more than 300 people in eight states in the South sucked up countless numbers of precious, irreplaceable family photos and documents and scattered them up to 200 miles from the homes from which they had been ripped.

Within a few hours of the disaster, a woman named Patty Bullion—whose home in Lester, Alabama, had been slightly damaged but was spared the full wrath of the killer winds—made a heartrending discovery. "I walked out the door and I saw something white lying outside in the road," she said. "I flipped it over and it was an ultrasound picture. It just ripped my heart out. I'm a Mom. I've got three kids. I can't imagine losing these items."[10] Within a few minutes she and her family had recov-

Former "Friends" Fight in Court

Late in 2002 Harvard University students Cameron and Tyler Winkelvoss, along with classmate Divya Narendra, began planning what they believed would be a better method of social interaction at Harvard and eventually other universities. They called their idea HarvardConnection. After several programmers did the initial work, late in 2003 the three turned to yet another Harvard student, Mark Zuckerberg, to complete the project.

Opinions differ as to what happened, but it seems clear that Zuckerberg developed a new application early the following year called thefacebook.com while leaving HarvardConnection incomplete. The Winkelvosses were upset. They tried to stop Zuckerberg from proceeding with his new application, which he later renamed Facebook. He refused. That began a lengthy court battle. In 2008 the Winkelvosses settled with Zuckerberg, accepting $20 million—later increased to $65 million—and Facebook stock. Three years later they filed another lawsuit that sought to overturn the 2008 decision. The twins said that Facebook had misrepresented the company's actual value. The 9th US District Court of Appeals disagreed with them. The judges said that the Winklevosses knew enough at the time of the settlement to make an informed decision and dismissed the lawsuit.

ered several more photos. Bullion set up a Facebook group, "Pictures and Documents found after the April 27, 2011 Tornadoes." Her expectations were modest. She thought the group might attract 100 people, and she would have been satisfied if it resulted in the return of one photo.

Bullion was successful far beyond her wildest imagination. Hundreds of people used it to post pictures and documents the storm had sent their way. Many more used the page to share their feelings about the tragedy. In less than two weeks, more than 100,000 people "liked" the page. That means they showed their approval of what had been posted.

Most important, scores of people found precious mementos on the site and reclaimed them. One of the most poignant photos showed Elvin

Patterson, a Mississippi grandfather, and his beloved dog Yoyo. Patterson was killed in the storm, which also destroyed his home and left nothing for his grieving relatives to remember him by. The photo turned up in a parking lot in Tennessee, 175 miles away. Within moments of its posting, Patterson's granddaughter Emily Washburn saw it and arranged to get it for her family.

Rapid Rise

These episodes are just two examples of the enormous influence of contemporary social media. According to estimates, Facebook has about 550 million members worldwide, while Twitter has passed the 200 million mark. While teens and young adults remain the heaviest users of social media, older adults are substantially increasing their participation. According to a report by the Pew Internet and American Life Project, the number of American adults aged 18–29 using the Internet who also belong to one or more social networks increased from 67 percent to 86 percent between May 2008 and May 2010, an increase of about 28 percent. In the same interval, the 30–49 age group underwent an increase of nearly 150 percent. The growth was even more spectacular among those aged 50–64 (more than 325 percent) and 65 and older (270 percent).

> "Ideas on Facebook have the ability to rush through groups and make many people aware of something almost simultaneously, spreading from one person to another and on to many with unique ease—like a virus." [12]
>
> — David Kirkpatrick, *Facebook Effect* author.

The Bin Laden and tornado episodes also indicate the distance that social media have traveled in just a few years. One of the tornado victims noted wistfully that he wished something similar could have been put in place after Hurricane Katrina in 2005. That would have been impossible. While Facebook existed, it was still largely confined to college campuses. And on September 11, 2001, television, radio, and traditional print media were the primary means by which people learned about the terrorist attacks in New York and Washington, DC. Much of the television coverage that day consisted of showing the same visual images over and over.

In fact, online communication and social networking as we know them today were still in relative infancy at the time of 9/11. While social networking itself is as old as human civilization, many people today refer to the "wired world," one in which communication is instantaneous.

This wired world began in the 1830s with the invention of the telegraph. Operators tapped out messages in Morse code and sent them out over wires. An operator at the other end decoded the messages and distributed them to the recipients. The invention of the telephone half a century later enabled people to communicate instantly, linked by telephone wires. Guglielmo Marconi's invention of the wireless telegraph in the early 1900s did away with wires altogether.

Continuing Development

The next step came with the rise of cumbersome commercial computers in the 1950s, which led to the development of personal computers in the 1970s. E-mail, which originated as a means of communication between defense institutions and universities, experienced explosive growth with the establishment of subscription-based companies such as Compuserve in the late 1980s and America Online (AOL) in the early 1990s. E-mail became even more popular when free services such as Hotmail and Yahoo! Mail came on the scene a few years later. The 1998 hit movie *You've Got Mail*, starring Tom Hanks and Meg Ryan, put Hollywood's stamp of approval on the revolution in online communication.

The World Wide Web (WWW) became publicly available in 1991 and greatly simplified access to the Internet. Commercial networks and websites began sprouting up to take advantage of this newfound accessibility. The first social networking site was Six Degrees, founded in 1997. Friendster (2002) and MySpace (2003) soon followed. Mark Zuckerberg established Facebook in his Harvard University dorm room in 2004, and Twitter came along in 2006.

Another key development was the evolution of cell phones from being simply a method of conversing without the constraints of landlines, to multipurpose devices such as iPhones that include cameras, games, Internet access, and many other features. Many people—especially teenagers and those in their twenties—now buy cell phones primarily because

Online Activities by Age

Ages 18–33	Ages 34–45	Ages 46–55	Ages 56–64	Ages 65–73	Ages 74+
E-mail	E-mail	E-mail	E-mail	E-mail	E-mail
Search	Search	Search	Search	Search	Search
Health info	Health info	Health info	Health info	Health info	Health info
Social network sites	Get news	Get news	Get news	Get news	Buy a product
Watch video	Gov't website	Gov't website	Gov't website	Travel reservations	Get news
Get news	Travel reservations	Travel reservations	Buy a product	Buy a product	Travel reservations
Buy a product	Watch video	Buy a product	Travel reservations	Gov't website	Gov't website
IM	Buy a product	Watch video	Bank online	Watch video	Bank online
Listen to music	Social network sites	Bank online	Watch video	Financial info	Financial info
Travel reservations	Bank online	Social network sites	Social network sites	Bank online	Religious info
Online classifieds	Online classifieds	Online classifieds	Online classifieds	Rate things	Watch video
Bank online	Listen to music	Listen to music	Financial info	Social network sites	Play games
Gov't website	IM	Financial info	Rate things	Online classifieds	Online classifieds
Play games	Play games	IM	Listen to music	IM	Social network sites
Read blogs	Financial info	Religious info	Religious info	Religious info	Rate things
Financial info	Religious info	Rate things	IM	Play games	Read blogs
Rate things	Read blogs	Read blogs	Play games	Listen to music	Donate to charity
Religious info	Rate things	Play games	Read blogs	Read blogs	Listen to music
Online auction	Online auction	Online auction	Online auction	Donate to charity	Podcasts
Podcasts	Donate to charity	Donate to charity	Donate to charity	Online auction	Online auction
Donate to charity	Podcasts	Podcasts	Podcasts	Podcasts	Blog
Blog	Blog	Blog	Blog	Blog	IM
Virtual worlds	Virtual worlds	Virtual worlds	Virtual worlds	Virtual worlds	Virtual worlds

Source: Pew Internet & American Life Project, "Generations 2010: What Different Generations Do Online," December 16, 2010. www.pewinternet.org.

14

of the ease, speed, and fun of texting. Cell phones also opened up the Internet to many people who might not have access to a computer.

Many Advantages

For many people, especially tweens and teens, social networking and online communication have become virtually indispensable elements of their daily lives. Online communication has several obvious advantages. Like phone calls, reception is instantaneous, with the additional benefit that recipients have the opportunity to mull over what they say and can even reconsider a hasty answer before replying. It is also convenient. E-mails are accessible at any time and can be printed out to provide a permanent record of conversations. Unlike phone calls, e-mails cannot be misheard. This can be especially advantageous in dealing with people with heavy accents or suffering from colds. Online conferencing, or webinars, allow people in widely separated areas to communicate without the necessity and expense of long plane flights.

Contemporary social media provide an easy way of keeping in touch with a wide variety of people. Rather than contacting everyone individually, a few moments allow users to update information to hundreds or thousands of people. It is also a good way of quickly and efficiently getting reliable information from a network of friends about almost anything, from local recreational sites for kids to the best clothing to wear on a vacation. Virtual dating services introduce people who probably would never meet otherwise. For people confined to their homes due to illness or injury, social media provide an easy way of staying in touch with the outside world.

In the business world, social media offer jobseekers an easy, convenient way of staying on top of available openings and provide potential employers with a richer palette of information than the traditional job application. They also offer many advantages for businesses, allowing them to position themselves in ways that traditional methods did not allow and at a fraction of the cost. Individual artists such as authors and musicians can promote themselves using social media tools such as Facebook and YouTube to reach a far wider audience and thereby increase sales. In turn, fans can interact with their favorite artists.

The Flip Side of Sports Fame

Professional athletes have taken advantage of social media, and many have thousands of Twitter followers. Their popularity—and more—can evaporate almost instantly with an ill-timed Tweet or two. For example, after Osama bin Laden's death, Pittsburgh Steelers running back Rashard Mendenhall Tweeted, "What kind of person celebrates death? It's amazing how people can HATE a man they have never even heard speak. We've only heard one side." He also seemed to question some of the events of 9/11.

Mendenhall's comments unleashed a firestorm of criticism from fans and others still rejoicing in Bin Laden's death. Steelers president Art Rooney II quickly distanced himself: "It is hard to explain or even comprehend what [Mendenhall] meant with his recent Twitter comments. The entire Steelers' organization is very proud of the job our military personnel have done and we can only hope this leads to our troops coming home soon."

Quoted in Sean Leahy, "Steelers Speak Out After Rashard Mendenhall's Critical Bin Laden Comments," *USA Today*, May 3, 2011. http://content.usatoday.com.

There appears to be a solid biological basis for this popularity. "In our evolutionary history, those who maintained large social networks could rely on them for resources, advice, and help that were vital for survival," points out noted theoretical physicist Michio Kaku. "The only difference today is that the magnitude of this tribal gossip has been multiplied enormously by mass media and can now circle the earth many times over within a fraction of a second."[11]

Facebook Effect

One of the most significant aspects of the new methods of communication is what author David Kirkpatrick calls the Facebook Effect. According to Kirkpatrick, the Facebook Effect occurs when people come into electronic contact with each other because of their mutual interest in a cause, an experience, or some sort of problem. Its scale is virtually unlimited, from a relative handful of people to millions. "Facebook's software makes information viral," he says. "Ideas on Facebook have the ability to rush through groups and make many people aware of something almost simultaneously, spreading from one person to another and on to many with unique ease—like a virus."[12]

In the past, this rapid spread of information depended on traditional media. During the 1960s, Americans were horrified by graphic images that appeared on television and in newspapers of fire hoses, baton-wielding policemen, and vicious dogs being turned on African Americans in the South who were conducting peaceful demonstrations for equal rights. The outrage led to passage of laws guaranteeing those rights.

The Facebook Effect—coupled with other new forms of social media and online communication such as cell phones, YouTube, and Twitter—empowers ordinary citizens to initiate this rapid spread of information. These citizens may provide coverage of events—sometimes within minutes or hours after they happen—that traditional media ignore or cannot cover for various reasons.

Take James Tate of Shelton, Connecticut. One night in early May 2011, he and his friends climbed ladders on the side of his high school and hung a sign inviting classmate Sonali Rodrigues to the senior prom. The headmaster, Beth Smith, was not amused. Acting in accordance with school rules regarding trespassing and the safety risks, she suspended Tate for a day. The timing of the suspension meant he could not go to the prom even though the girl he had asked said "yes" to his invitation.

As journalist Peter Applebome observed, "Before Twitter, Facebook, Tumblr and the rest, this might not have been enough to turn Mr. Tate's plight into an international cause célèbre. These days, however, it proved a natural, and Mr. Tate's story has quickly become a morality play of crime and punishment and love's labour's lost."[13]

The Twittersphere went viral with Tweets that supported Tate and attacked Smith. A Facebook page called "Let James Tate Go to the Prom" attracted nearly 200,000 "likes" within a week and generated several spinoff pages, such as "James Tate for Prom King 2011" and "James Tate Thanks You." The virtual commotion led to Tate appearing on the *Today*

Show and *Jimmy Kimmel Live*. Citing the extraordinary pressure, Smith relented. Tate and Rodrigues were prom-bound.

Saving Lives

Besides saving prom dates, social media can save lives. A young American cell phone gaming engineer of South Asian extraction named Sameer Bhatia contracted a deadly form of leukemia in 2007. Only a bone marrow transplant could save him. None of his relatives and friends could provide the match he needed. Doctors felt that his best hope lay with other South Asians, but with only a relative handful of people in this ethnic group in the national bone-marrow database his chances did not look good.

Bhatia's business partner launched an e-mail campaign among people they knew personally, who in turn forwarded the information to their friends. Facebook pages and YouTube videos quickly sprang up, resulting in the addition of nearly 25,000 South Asians to the database. One was a match, and Bhatia received the transplant he needed.

Sadly, the disease was too advanced. Bhatia died in 2008. But his death was hardly in vain. Within a short time the new additions to the database resulted in 266 other transplants among South Asians. And a Stanford University professor named Jennifer Aaker was so inspired by Bhatia's story that she wrote *The Dragonfly Effect: Quick, Effective, and Powerful Ways to Use Social Media to Drive Social Change*, a practical guide showing how virtually anyone can harness the power of social media to effect beneficial changes in society.

Social media can even help ease the frustration of being stuck in traffic. When his car broke down on a busy freeway during the morning commute and traffic immediately began backing up, driver Michael Micheletti sent out a Tweet: "That black BMW stalled in the center lane of I-5? Yeah, that's me. Sorry, I don't like it either."[14] A number of people re-Tweeted his message, the state department of transportation issued an alert—and Micheletti acquired a number of new followers on his Twitter account.

Widening the Playing Field

Professional sports teams have been quick to take advantage of social media. The Seattle Sounders of Major League Soccer set league atten-

Major League Soccer's Seattle Sounders attribute their consistent fan base and sold-out games to online social networking. Pictured is a member of the Sounders (in green) battling with his opponent for the ball in a 2011 match.

dance records in their first year of existence in 2009 and consistently sell out their home games. A primary reason is the team's 155,000 Facebook friends and 13,000 Twitter followers. The development of a strong regional rivalry in 2011 from nearby Vancouver, British Columbia, and Portland, Oregon—both of which also have strong social network systems—is likely to maintain high attendance levels.

"Today, all three clubs, indeed all the teams in M.L.S., are putting bricks and mortar on the ground and more ethereal foundations in cyberspace," notes sportswriter Jack Bell of the *New York Times*. "Social media is an important resource; the clubs have fostered and encouraged fan involvement by the Timbers Army, the Vancouver Southsiders and Seattle's five independent supporters groups."[15] Vancouver team president Bob Lenarduzzi echoes Bell: "We're taking several thousand fans to Seattle and the social media has made it much easier for them to organize."[16]

The National Football League has been among the most social media–savvy sports organizations. Like the Oscars, it encouraged two-screen activity during Super Bowl XLV on NFL.com. Advertisers got into the act by releasing their highly anticipated commercials several days early, then encouraging viewers to comment via Twitter and Facebook in real time on game day to get the most bang from their 3-million-bucks-per-minute investment.

> "We're taking several thousand fans to Seattle and the social media has made it much easier for them to organize." [16]
>
> — Vancouver, BC, soccer team president Bob Lenarduzzi.

However, NFL officials cannot have been happy when labor negotiations between the players and owners broke down a month later and the players quickly began Tweeting to make sure that fans got their point of view. With nearly 40 percent of them having active Twitter accounts—led by Chad Ochocinco of the Cincinnati Bengals with 1.7 million followers—there was no lack of an audience.

Players Cautioned to Take Care

The players union even issued a statement to its members: "In this modern world of media and social networking, know that the nature of comments you make on Facebook, Twitter and text are taken seriously by the public. One negative comment by a player can be detrimental to the negotiation process and confuse the public and media on the position of our players."[17]

The National Basketball Association has been particularly successful in positioning itself. In addition to online video, smartphone apps—some of which allow live streaming—and social media gaming, NBA officials say that their league has more than 100 million Twitter followers and Facebook "likes" for the league, its teams, and players. NBA.com, the official website, claims more than 2 billion video views. In February, 2011, the league released a Facebook game called NBA Legend, which allows users to create virtual players and play simulated games. It quickly gained more than a million users.

As these and seemingly countless other examples illustrate, new uses emerge on almost a daily basis as a result of perceived need and technological advances. But the flexibility of social media can almost be too much of a good thing. For many people, trying to keep up with everyone with whom they have a connection of some sort can result in an inundation of updates. But this situation can be controlled. It may take a while, but most users eventually strike a balance and find a way to stay in touch with the ones who mean the most to them.

Chapter Two

Social Networking Takes to the Streets

At first glance, a malnourished 4-year-old boy in the steaming jungles of Colombia, a 26-year-old fruit and vegetable vendor in a small town in Tunisia, and a 28-year-old businessman in Alexandria, Egypt, would not seem to be obvious candidates to serve as centerpieces of social upheavals. But the rise of social media catapulted these otherwise obscure figures into prominence and led to significant changes in their respective countries.

One primary reason is the almost explosive growth of social networking sites such as Facebook and Twitter outside the United States. In 2008 Facebook users were divided about 50-50 between the United States and other countries. Two years later, foreign accounts had soared to 70 percent of the total while American Facebook users doubled between 2009 and 2010. Twitter's foreign expansion has been even more rapid. Between June 2009 and April 2010, foreign accounts increased from 45 percent to a whopping 63 percent.

Vital Sources of Information

In many countries the government rigidly controls the news media, and voices of dissent are almost never heard. Even in cases of a more open press, threats and intimidation can result in less-than-adequate reporting. As a result, online social media have assumed a large role in providing vital information to citizens—and to the world.

For example, Colombia had been plagued by the Revolutionary Armed Forces of Colombia (FARC) for nearly five decades. Though professing to be on the side of the country's impoverished peasants, FARC has long been considered a terrorist organization because of its kidnappings, assassinations, torture tactics, and involvement in the narcotics trade. Most Colombians hated and feared FARC but felt powerless to do anything—to say nothing of fearing for their safety if they decided to speak out.

In 2002 FARC kidnapped Colombian presidential candidate Ingrid Betancourt and a top aide, Clara Rojas, and subjected them to a lengthy captivity. During this time, Rojas gave birth to a son, Emmanuel. In December 2007 President Hugo Chavez of neighboring Venezuela brokered a deal with FARC to release Emmanuel, his mother, and another hostage. Colombians rejoiced. But as the days went by with no sign of Emmanuel, the nation's ardor turned to anxiety—then to anger with the revelation that FARC did not even have Emmanuel. He had become seriously ill nearly two years previously because of the poor quality of his diet. FARC guerrillas took him from his mother and gave him to a peasant family who had no idea of his parentage. This family eventually turned him over to a government-run health clinic.

At the time of this stunning revelation, a Colombian named Oscar Morales was vacationing with his family. Like his countrymen, Morales was concerned about the fate of Emmanuel and the hundreds of other hostages, many of whom had been held for years. When Morales learned of FARC's duplicity about Emmanuel, he was outraged. "We felt assaulted by the FARC," he said. "How could they dare negotiate for the life of a child they didn't even have. People felt this was too much. How much longer was FARC going to play with us and lie to us?"[18]

He wanted to do something. Already a frequent Facebook user, he typed "FARC" into the search box. Nothing came up. The guerrillas had in effect cowed the entire country. No one seemed to want to say anything that might place themselves in FARC's crosshairs.

Speaking Out Against Fear

Morales was a civil engineer, not a militant. Yet with no one else willing to step up, he decided it was time to take action. He created a Facebook group known as "One Million Voices Against FARC." Its symbol was a logo that turned the Colombian flag vertically and superimposed four phrases on it: NO MORE KIDNAPPINGS, NO MORE LIES, NO MORE KILLINGS, NO MORE FARC in increasingly larger lettering.

Shortly after midnight on January 4, 2008, Morales launched his new group. It was public, so anyone could join. He sent invitations to his 100 friends and went to bed. When he woke up the next morning, his organization had 1,500 members. By late afternoon, the number was at 4,000. Two days later, that number had doubled and showed no sign of slowing down. Morales had touched a sensitive nerve. Facebook member discussion boards buzzed with calls for action.

Soon afterward FARC released Clara Rojas, and she was reunited with Emmanuel. To Morales and his thousands of new allies, the gesture did not matter. The apparent game that FARC had played with the boy tapped into the pent-up anger the nation had endured for decades, and One Million Voices Against FARC provided an outlet. "We want the world to know we're tired," said a 21-year-old Colombian woman. "What the FARC has done is just the limit."[19]

Taking to the Streets

Morales and other people who had stepped up to take leading voices in the burgeoning group decided to organize a public demonstration on February 4, 2011, called the National March against FARC. That was not all. More than a million Colombians had fled the country in previous years due to FARC terror and now lived in cities such as Miami, Los Angeles, and Paris. They also wanted to take part and scheduled demonstrations in their respective cities on the same day. What was especially remarkable was how many people in Colombia had joined the movement, using their own names in spite of the risk of reprisals. Their courage emboldened many more to join.

On the day of the demonstration, it is estimated that nearly 10 million Colombians took part inside the country, with another 2 million participating in more than 150 cities worldwide. In Morales's home city of Barranquilla, more than 300,000 turned out, more than six times his most optimistic estimate. In terms of overall numbers, it was the largest antiterrorism demonstration in history.

Thousands of people joined a campaign on Facebook calling for Colombian rebels to release hostage Clara Rojas. Rojas, released after about six years in captivity, waves to supporters upon returning to Bogotá in January 2008.

FARC remains in existence and still holds hundreds of hostages. But the existence of One Million Voices provides those hostages with hope. According to Betancourt (who was freed in a commando operation later in 2008), "I think the press has been astonishing. That kept me alive. That kept my fellow hostages alive. And it's keeping the ones who are still in the jungle alive."[20] It also appears that FARC's numbers have decreased significantly. "Internet and especially social media is an amazing tool to communicate in real time," Morales says. "Social media breaks boundaries and is one global channel, one global network. This is the beauty of internet—we can organise things together globally."[21]

Tired of Being Harassed

Morales's words were borne out in Tunisia late in 2010. Ever since the age of 10, 26-year-old Mohamed Bouazizi had been his family's primary source of support. His father died when Bouazizi was three. His stepfather was in poor health and often unable to work. His older brother moved away. So almost every day, Bouazizi piled his heavy wooden cart with vegetables, then pushed it to the marketplace in his hometown of Sidi Bouzid. According to his aunt, he had just one aspiration: to be able to buy a small truck. "Not to cruise around in, but for his work," she explains. "He would come home tired after pushing the cart around all day. All he wanted was a pickup."[22]

"Internet and especially social media is an amazing tool to communicate in real time."[21]

— Oscar Morales, founder of One Million Voices Against FARC.

He probably had another aspiration: to be left alone. Almost every day, police officers and other town officials harassed him. Sometimes they took away the scales he used to weigh his produce. At other times they confiscated the produce itself. Or he might be fined for not having a permit, an expense he could ill afford.

On December 17, 2010, he loaded up his cart and went to work as usual. And as usual, he encountered harassment. According to reports, a policewoman ordered him to surrender his scales. He refused. She slapped him, then called on several policemen for assistance. After wrestling him to the ground, they swaggered away with his scale and his produce. Deeply humiliated, Bouazizi sought recourse at his town's municipal building. Officials were too busy to meet with him, he was told.

Googling in the Gulf

In the Persian Gulf nation of Bahrain, most of the population consists of Shiite Muslims. The country's ruling family and close associates are Sunni Muslims. Late in November, 2006, members of the country's Shiite population began using Google Earth to see the distribution of land in their country. They were shocked to see immense tracts of empty or near-empty land—more than 90 percent of the country—and vast, sprawling palaces belonging to Sunnis while the Shiites were packed tightly together. "We are 17 people crowded in one small house, like many people in the southern district," said one Shiite. "And you see on Google how many palaces there are and how the al-Khalifas [the Sunni ruling family] have the rest of the country to themselves."

The images spread quickly among the Shiites. Sensing their anger, the ruling party blocked Google Earth—even though this action was illegal, according to the country's constitution. The Shiites, however, made a PDF file of the images to keep them in circulation. The discontent simmered until early 2011, when the Shiite Bahrainis rose in protest along with much of the rest of the Arab world. The government fought back savagely, killing and wounding many of them.

Quoted in Thomas Friedman, "This Is Just the Start," *New York Times*, March 1, 2011. www.nytimes.com.

He went to a nearby store, purchased some fuel, returned to the municipal building, doused himself, and lit a match. Twenty-three days later, Tunisia's longtime ruler, Zine el Abidine ben Ali, left the country after a virtually nonstop series of street demonstrations that Bouazizi's protest engendered.

The Viral Power of Video

Bouazizi was not the first young Tunisian to immolate himself in protest against high unemployment and other negative social conditions in the country. The difference was that later that day, as the young man lay heavily bandaged in a local hospital, two of his relatives—Rochdi Horchani and Ali Bouazizi—filmed a peaceful protest that his mother led and posted it on Facebook. That evening *Al Jazeera*, the Arab news network, replayed the video. People all over Tunisia were incensed, and street protests throughout the country began.

Tunisian authorities fought back, trying to suppress the inflammatory footage. They had a great deal of experience in this area. Even though government officials often describe Tunisia as a democracy, the government routinely censors material on the Internet and imprisons those who speak out. According to the Society to Protect Journalists, Tunisia is one of the ten worst countries in which to blog. Ben Ali's increasingly desperate government tried to stem the flow of information—beginning with power blackouts. Authorities tried to cut off access to the Internet and to keep people from using Facebook. When those measures failed, they began arresting people.

Unlike previous instances, this time Tunisians figured out how to circumvent government intervention. A third of the 3.6 million people in Tunisia have Internet access, one of the highest rates in all of Africa, and nearly half of those belong to Facebook. Even though many were afraid to even post "Like" on their Facebook pages, an increasing number of videos continued to be posted. In a revolution that Horchani termed "a rock in one hand, a cell phone in the other,"[23] more and more Tunisians became emboldened. The protesters continued to post videos and coordinate further protests. Facebook and Twitter played key roles in this effort. Twitter spokeswoman Carolyn Penner said, "We sit back and watch in awe at how people are using Twitter and other platforms to provide on-the-ground perspective during this highly developing and potentially historical moment."[24] A photo of Ben Ali visiting Bouazizi in his hospital room received widespread coverage. It further fanned the flames of dissent on the grounds that the visit was far too late, and the only reason for it was to cut off dissent. Bouazizi died on January 4, 2011. Ben Ali fled

> "We sit back and watch in awe at how people are using Twitter and other platforms to provide on-the-ground perspective during this highly developing and potentially historical moment."[24]
>
> — Twitter spokeswoman Carolyn Penner.

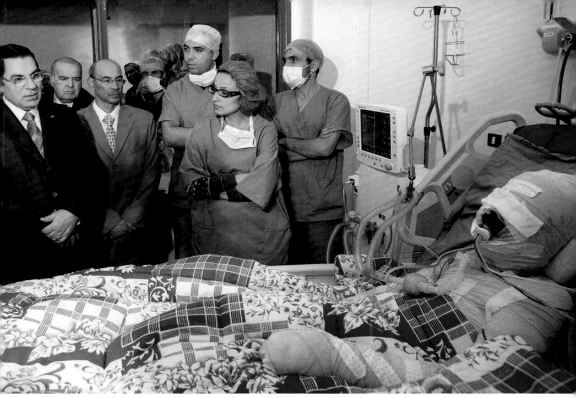

Tunisian president Zine el Abidine ben Ali visits a heavily bandaged Mohamed Bouazizi in the hospital. When police confiscated the produce that supported Bouazizi and his family, he lit himself on fire. The photo and accounts of life in Tunisia spread through online social media, sparking a revolution that led to Ben Ali's downfall.

Tunisia and went into exile a few days later—an outcome that virtually no one could have foreseen or predicted a month earlier.

According to journalist Roger Cohen, this outcome came about because "Bouazizi exploded at the indignity of having his vegetable cart confiscated. He exploded at humiliation. He could not tolerate being a pawn—and a penniless one. His act was small but he gave as much as anyone can give—his life. And because of his times, because Facebook and Al Jazeera exist, his death reverberated."[25]

Unrest Spreads to Egypt

The reverberations soon expanded to Egypt, nearly a thousand miles across the Sahara Desert but just a mouse click away in cyberspace and where nearly half the population lives on the equivalent of a few dollars

A Teenage Martyr

One example of Syrian activists' success in making the world aware of the ghastly situation in their country came in late May 2011. A month earlier, 13-year-old Hamza Ali al-Khateeb—who enjoyed raising homing pigeons and swimming in nearby irrigation channels—tagged along when his family went to a demonstration in the town of Saida. Government troops opened fire. Hamza was separated from his family and captured by security forces. A month later, they returned his corpse to his family.

According to *New York Times* columnist David Brooks, "While in custody, he had apparently been burned, beaten, lacerated and given electroshocks. His jaw and kneecaps were shattered. He was shot in both arms. When his father saw the state of Hamza's body, he passed out." Videos were smuggled out of Syria and posted on YouTube. Within a few days, a Facebook page called We Are All Hamza Ali al-Khateeb—a deliberate echo of the potent We Are All Khalid Said page that helped incite the revolution in Egypt—had more than 60,000 followers. As protests continued despite brutal government attacks, many people carried posters with the boy's image.

David Brooks, "The Depravity Factor," *New York Times*, June 2, 2011. www.nytimes.com.

a day. President Hosni Mubarak had been in power even longer than Ben Ali and oversaw a security apparatus that made the country a virtual police state. A series of self-immolations began on January 17, 2011, and antigovernment activists announced plans for a nationwide day of anger on January 25. Egyptian activist Mohamed ElBaradei, winner of the 2005 Nobel Peace Prize for his work as director general of the International Atomic Energy Agency, warned, "What has transpired in Tunisia is no surprise and should be very instructive both for the political elite in Egypt and those in the west that back dictatorships."[26]

ElBaradei's words proved to be prophetic. Over the next few days, more than 85,000 people responded to a "Revolution Day" page on

Facebook, which presented a list of demands to the Mubarak regime. They pledged to appear in person at the January 25 rally. In turn, they were encouraged to pass the word to their friends. It helped that more than one-fifth of the population had Internet access. Egypt also had nearly 4.5 million Facebook users, more than in any other country in Africa.

The Story of Khalid Said

It was hardly Facebook's first foray into Egyptian politics. The previous May, Wael Ghonim, a Google executive based in nearby Dubai, had volunteered to run ElBaradei's Facebook fan page with its emphasis on voting and democratic reform. He wrote that "Once you are a fan, whatever we publish gets on your wall. So the government has NO way to block it later. Unless they block Facebook altogether."[27]

The following month, Ghonim's involvement in Egyptian politics became much deeper when he learned of the death of a 28-year-old man named Khalid Said in Alexandria. According to the official police report, Said was a known drug dealer who died following his arrest on June 6 when he tried to swallow a bag of marijuana.

A vastly different picture soon emerged that gave the lie to the official report. Said's only "crime" was receiving, most likely by accident, a video of police officers exchanging seized drugs and cash. He forwarded the video to a few friends, who in turn forwarded it to their friends. Several weeks later, two officers who had appeared in the video seized Said at an Internet café and, after handcuffing him, began smashing his face against a marble table. The café owner protested, so the officers took Said outside and continued the assault, slamming him against steel steps and kicking him when he collapsed to the ground.

The following day his parents were notified that he had died. Suspicious of the official account, they bribed a guard at the morgue to take a photo of Said's body. The ghastly image of Said's distorted face, with its broken jaw, missing teeth and multiple abrasions was in stark contrast to photos taken before his capture, which showed a handsome, almost serene young man looking optimistically toward his future. Coupled with his broken ribs, the photo clearly revealed that his death was not due to choking on a bag of marijuana.

The Power of Social Media

As was the case with Mohamed Bouazizi, social media prevented Said from becoming simply another statistic of a corrupt regime. The photos were posted on the Internet, where they quickly went viral, and prompted Ghonim to begin a new Facebook page called "We Are All Khalid Said" soon afterward. It became one of the leading Egyptian Facebook protest sites. As journalist Mike Giglio observes, "The page quickly became a forceful campaign against police brutality in Egypt, with a constant stream of photos, videos and news. Ghonim's interactive style combined with the page's carefully calibrated posts and it eventually became the vehicle to promote the January 25 protest."[28] On the appointed day, hundreds of thousands of protesters swarmed into Tahrir Square in Cairo, Egypt's capital city. The demonstrators included Ghonim, as well as Khalid Said's mother and sister.

The Egyptian government fought back. On January 27 it cut off cell phone and Internet services. Police arrested Ghonim, though he had already made arrangements for the page to continue. "We Are All Wael Ghonim" Facebook pages began to emerge. The police released him, virtually unharmed, two weeks later.

The protests continued unabated in the face of sometimes violent government attempts to suppress them. Unlike Tunisia, where mainstream media had been slow to pick up on the protests, these demonstrations were conducted in the full glare of international media coverage from the beginning and attracted hundreds of thousands of participants every day. Tahrir Square, previously unknown to much of the world, became perhaps the most famous piece of real estate on the globe. State-run Egyptian television tried to lessen the impact by running old broadcasts showing a nearly empty square. Few people were fooled.

Washington Post reporter Ernesto Londono noted,

> Had it not been for a leaked morgue photo of his mangled corpse, tenacious relatives and the power of Facebook, the death of Khaled Said would have become a footnote in the annals of Egyptian police brutality. Instead, outrage over the beating death of the 28-year-old man in this coastal city last summer, and attempts by local authorities to cover it up, helped spark the mass protests demanding the ouster of Egyptian President Hosni Mubarak.[29]

Said's uncle Ali Kassem added, "Every family in Egypt has seen something like this happen to a member. I will feel like I have attained justice only if the regime falls and a new government is formed."[30]

Kassem's wish was fulfilled on February 11, 2011, when Mubarak announced that he would step down. Soon the grisly image of Said's battered and broken face was replaced on his Facebook page by a drawing of a smiling woman with a background of colorful blossoms holding an equally happy baby waving an Egyptian flag with the legend "Dreams Come True."

Other Protests

Tunisia and Egypt were not the only countries where people wanted freedom from longtime autocratic rulers. In many other countries in the Middle East, people—often using Twitter, Facebook, YouTube, and other social media to organize and get the word out to the rest of the world—rose up in what has been called the "Arab Spring."

Wael Ghonim, a Google executive, stands with his arm raised at the center of an antigovernment protest in Egypt in 2011. Ghonim launched a campaign on Facebook to protest corruption in Egypt's government and the mistreatment of Egyptian citizens.

For example, protests erupted in Syria in March 2011. President Bashar al-Assad ordered troops to fire on their own people, killing hundreds and wounding even more. Protesters were arrested and thrown in jail, where brutal beatings were common. Syrians who peacefully attended funerals for the fallen were often attacked, further inflating the casualty lists.

> "Had it not been for a leaked morgue photo of his mangled corpse, tenacious relatives and the power of Facebook, the death of Khaled Said would have become a footnote in the annals of Egyptian police brutality."[29]
>
> — Journalist Ernesto Londono.

With Assad clamping down on news media—both foreign and domestic—the only way of getting the word out was through an underground system of Syrian activists in exile. Many had fled the country to avoid capture and almost certain execution, then smuggled cell phones and cameras into the country. They coordinated the release of the ensuing videos to ensure that the world was fully aware of what was happening. Joshua Landis, a professor of Middle East studies at the University of Oklahoma, says, "These activists have completely flipped the balance of power on the regime, and that's all due to social media."[31]

Oscar Morales would seem to agree with this assessment. In a recent speech he noted, "As recent events in the Middle East demonstrate, social media has become a powerful tool of democracy. Here and elsewhere, citizens are speaking out and demanding to participate in conversations about their freedom. Social media has revolutionized the medium and is spreading the message."[32]

Chapter Three

Online Perils
and Pitfalls

Despite all the advantages and benefits of rapid online communication and social media, they have a dark side. Like any tools, they have the potential for abuse and misuse. As famed American author Mark Twain noted, "A lie can run around the world six times while the truth is still trying to put on its pants."[33] Because of the speed and extensiveness of social networking, assertions of dubious accuracy can be posted and almost instantly go viral, thereby requiring considerable effort to correct. Sometimes the truth never emerges. In either case, temporary or even permanent damage to the reputation of people, groups, or institutions can occur.

Privacy is another concern. Anything people post instantly goes into the public realm and may stay there for weeks, months, or even years. In their zeal to post pictures of a raunchy party when they were 16, they may not realize that those shots could come back to haunt them in 5 or 10 years. Accordingly, the rise of online communication and social networking has resulted in a new set of perils for users.

Sexting

One of these new perils is a practice that has come to be known as sexting. The term first appeared around 2005 and represents a combination of "sex" and "texting." In practice, it means sending risqué or pornographic pictures between computers and/or mobile phones, usually accompanied by textual comments. Sexting is legal, protected under First Amendment rights of free speech. But once a sext has been sent out, the person who originated the content cannot control who sees it. Something sent in confidence to a single person can be quickly disseminated to hundreds of people—or many more.

A recent case in Lacey, Washington, graphically illustrates the dangers. An eighth-grade girl named Jane (not her real name) took a full-length frontal nude photo of herself late in 2009 and sent it to her new boyfriend Jack (also not his real name). Not long afterward, they broke up. For some reason, Jack sent the photo to another girl, a classmate of theirs and a former friend of Jane. The two girls had argued about a boy (not Jack) and become enemies, though apparently Jack did not know about that situation.

This girl, Cindy (not her real name) did not hesitate. "Ho alert," she texted on her cell phone late that evening. "If you think this girl is a whore, then text this to all your friends."[34] She attached the photo and sent it to everyone on her call list. The recipients did what she asked. While no one knows exactly how many people saw the damaging photo, the numbers almost certainly ranged at least into the thousands—many of whom knew Jane personally.

Reaction came swiftly. Jane's cell phone began buzzing shortly after midnight. Some were from friends who had received Cindy's sext, warning her about the situation. Others were from boys who taunted her. School the next day was a nightmare. Jane was humiliated. School officials tried to contain the damage by confiscating students' cell phones.

Prosecuting attorney Rick Peters confronted Jack and Cindy. They were handcuffed and taken away. Jack spent a night in juvenile detention before being released. Peters threatened to charge them—as well as another girl who had been actively involved in sending out the sext—with distributing pornography. This charge is a felony which could have put them behind bars for nearly a year and forced them to register as sex offenders. He eventually decided to use the incident as a way of educating the community. The three teenagers agreed to perform community service, speaking out about the dangers of sexting.

More than a year later, the photo still haunted Jane, with jibes from strangers continuing to follow her. She said, "I guess if they are about to send a picture, and they have a feeling, like, they're not sure they should, then don't do it at all. I mean, what are you thinking? It's freaking stupid!"[35]

A member of the Connecticut state police cybercrimes unit conducts a seminar on the dangers of teen sexting. The idea of sending nude pictures to a friend's cell phone appeals to some teens even though it carries many risks.

The Appeal of Sexting

Stupid or not, sexting appeals to many young people. It is easy to do and may seem cool, making the people who are doing it seem particularly attractive. "Having a naked picture of your significant other on your cellphone is an advertisement that you're sexually active to a degree that gives you status," said Peters. "It's an electronic hickey."[36]

The appeal of sexting extends well beyond young people. While teen-agers may cringe at the thought of their parents or grandparents involved in anything having to do with sex, adults—even those well into their fifties and sixties—are sexting to an increasing degree. For couples, it is a way to interact in a more intimate way when one of them is traveling. It is also a form of flirting that may help make single adults feel younger and more exuberant. Sexting frees them from many of the inhibitions of in-person encounters or telephone calls. A 50-year-old divorced South

Carolina nurse, for example, notes that "it makes you a little more brave. . . . If you're sitting in a restaurant waiting for your food, you can just talk dirty to someone, and no one knows what you're doing."[37]

Of course, adult sexting has its own set of drawbacks. As is the case with teens, the image may be forwarded to many people. Another is that a sexter may create high expectations by sending a picture taken years or even decades previously and clearly different from his or her present appearance. A third is that parents or grandparents may let their youngsters use their cell phone, forgetting that it contains explicit images of themselves.

Cyberbullying

Cyberbullying is another example of the negative aspects of social media. While schoolyard bullies have been around for many years, new forms of communication, such as cell phones, text messaging, interactive games, and instant messages, have dramatically increased their reach and influence in both scope and intensity.

Fifteen-year-old Phoebe Prince and her family moved to South Hadley, Massachusetts, from their native Ireland in the fall of 2009. According to the family, one of the major reasons for moving was "so that Phoebe could experience America."[38] Unfortunately, Phoebe's "American experience" turned out to be tragically different from what they had in mind.

> "The investigation revealed relentless activity directed toward Phoebe, designed to humiliate her and to make it impossible for her to remain at school."[39]
>
> — District Attorney Elizabeth Scheibel.

Soon after their arrival, Phoebe—a high school freshman—briefly dated a senior football player. Almost immediately, she became the target of an onslaught of negative cell phone calls, e-mails, text messages, Facebook posts, and similar social media attacks in addition to verbal harassment in the school's halls. Finally she could not take it any longer. Phoebe hanged herself on January 14, 2010.

According to District Attorney Elizabeth Scheibel, who brought felony charges against nine South Hadley students, Phoebe's suicide was "the culmination of a nearly three-month campaign of verbally assaultive behavior and threats of physical harm. . . . The investigation revealed relentless

When Texting Kills Others

The cases of the two young Rochester (England) women dying in TWD (texting while driving) situations are tragic. But in both cases they were the only victims. Other TWD cases involve little or no harm to the driver while killing other people. In November 2006, 24-year-old Victoria McBryde had a tire blow out near Oxford, England. She flipped on her hazard lights and sat in her car, waiting for help to arrive. She texted a friend: "Can things get any worse?" They could.

Moments later, a car driven by Philippa Curtis slammed into Victoria's car. Victoria suffered fatal head injuries. Police determined that in less than 90 minutes of driving that evening, Curtis had sent or received more than 20 text messages. The lack of skid marks indicated that she was so engrossed in texting that she did not see Victoria's car before the fatal impact. Curtis suffered only minor scrapes and served just six months in prison. The effects on Victoria's family were far worse. "They say time heals but in reality it is like this bomb has exploded in the middle of this family and we are all left to pick up the pieces on our own," her mother said.

Quoted in Adam Luck, "Caution: Text Driver Ahead. How Texting While Driving Ended with Tragic Consequences for One Girl," *Daily Mail* (London), July 6, 2010. www.dailymail.co.uk.

activity directed toward Phoebe, designed to humiliate her and to make it impossible for her to remain at school. The bullying, for her, became intolerable."[39]

While Phoebe Prince's case is somewhat extreme, she is far from being the only young person who has suffered from this form of harassment. According to statistics from iSafe, a nonprofit education program dedicated to providing young people and adults with useful information about responsible Internet use, more than half of all teenagers have been subject to cyberbullying or acted as cyberbullies themselves. Boys and girls are about equally likely to be victims or perpetrators, though boys are more likely to be threatened with physical harm. And Phoebe is not the only young person driven to suicide by cyberbullying.

Not surprisingly, cyberbullying also extends to adults. An extreme form has surfaced in parts of the Arab world. Particularly in Iraq, many people receive threatening text messages, often numbering in the hundreds. Journalists are particular targets, as they report on controversial subjects. One journalist received a text that read, "Your tongue has become too big, and it is time to cut it off."[40] Another was told to stop reporting about a particular topic. "Otherwise, the outcome will be disastrous,"[41] the message read.

> "Your tongue has become too big, and it is time to cut it off."[40]
>
> — Anonymous text threat to Iraqi journalist.

Online Predators

Young people may be particularly at risk to online predators. According to the New Hampshire–based Crimes Against Children Research Center, at least one in five teenagers who regularly go online has received unwanted sexual solicitations. More than three-quarters of those solicitations are extended to ages 14 and over. A famous *New Yorker* magazine cartoon by Peter Steiner, which appeared in 1993, features a canine at a computer saying to a fellow four-legged friend, "On the Internet, nobody knows you're a dog."[42] The succeeding years have only served to increase the timeliness of the cartoon.

That is because online predators—virtually all of whom are adult males—find it increasingly easy to obtain crucial information about potential victims by cleverly disguising their true identity and posing as fellow teenagers as they prowl the Internet. Teens who complain about problems with parents and/or teachers are especially at risk. The predator can gain their trust by sympathizing with them and relating similar experiences (almost always fictitious). Even seemingly innocent pictures posted on Facebook or elsewhere can provide a wealth of information to those who know what to look for—the location of sporting events in which the potential victim participates, car license numbers, even home addresses.

Chat rooms are especially fruitful fields for predators. Cloaked in anonymity, they often pose as teens and engage in conversations with other teens that grow more intimate over time. The predator's goal is to convince his targets to meet him, often to have sex—even though it is illegal for adults to have sex with underage children. This goal can be surprisingly easy to achieve, as surveys have shown that only one in four teens might tell his or her parents about responding to an online solicitation.

Sometimes the predator is not seeking a personal encounter. After gaining the confidence of his victims, he may ask them to strip for a web camera. Then he threatens to post the videos unless the victim performs more explicit acts on camera.

Scammers and Swindlers

Not all social media problems involve the possibility of physical harm. Many legitimate businesses use the convenience and far-reaching nature of the Internet to advertise their products and services and interact with their customers. Unfortunately, scammers and swindlers take advantage of the same opportunities. Stories of people being taken advantage of financially through online hoaxes are legion.

Students hold a candlelight vigil for Phoebe Prince, a Massachusetts teenager who killed herself after being subjected to vicious cyberbullying.

According to the Internet Crime Complaint Center (IC3), a federal organization affiliated with the FBI, nearly half of all complaints come from people between the ages of 40 and 59. In 2009 the IC3 estimated a total loss of more than half a billion dollars from more than 300,000 victims, nearly double the loss from the previous year.

One common scam is frequently associated with African countries, most commonly Nigeria. Senders claim to be an important government official or lawyer in Nigeria and request the recipient's help in transferring a significant amount of money, which they claim is tied up in a bank account due to red tape. In return, they offer to send part of that money to the recipient as a reward for their help. Most people quickly delete such bogus offers. But a few are willing to go along with the idea. Soon the "official" says a problem has arisen and the recipient will need to send some money to resolve the situation. If the recipient is foolish enough to comply, soon another "problem" arises and leads to another request for funds. The hapless individuals who have begun with high hopes eventually realize that they will never see a single cent from their participation. In fact, their bank accounts may be completely cleaned out.

> **"On the Internet, nobody knows you're a dog."** [42]
>
> — *New Yorker* cartoonist Peter Steiner.

Some scammers may also claim to be dying of incurable illnesses and wish to donate their money to charity. They may appeal to the recipient's obvious "kindness," and offer them a portion of the funds for doing "God's work." The approach may be different but the outcome remains the same. The recipient winds up with nothing except a depleted bank account and—hopefully—the wisdom not to be sucked in again.

Other online hoaxes include "official notification" that the recipient has won a sweepstakes drawing or an outright request for donations to benefit a charity. Many computers have spam filters that detect such efforts at fraud, but some of these bogus messages still manage to get through. Common sense and the knowledge that something that sounds too good to be true is almost certainly not true, are the best defenses.

Using Social Media in Inappropriate Situations

Despite the obvious dangers, many people (particularly teens but also many adults) text while driving and in other situations in which they need to devote full attention to what they are doing. According to the US Department of Transportation (DOT), driving while distracted—primarily through any use of a cell phone or other wireless device—is a factor in more than one-fourth of all automobile accidents. The DOT identifies three primary distractions while driving: visual (taking your eyes off the road), manual (removing your hands from the wheel), and cognitive (thinking about something else besides driving). Texting is the worst offender because it involves all three. In addition, some studies equate cell phone usage with delaying reaction times by the same amount as a blood alcohol level of .08, the legal maximum in many states.

The case of Heather Lerch of the small town of Rochester, Washington—population about 2,000—shows the sometimes deadly consequences of texting while driving (TWD). Heather bought a new car for her 19th birthday in January 2010. Driving home one night about a month later, Heather decided to exchange text messages with a friend even though she was less than three miles from home. Moments later, she lost control of her car. It crashed through a guardrail. Heather died instantly.

Heather's parents were devastated. In their grief, they wanted to prevent other parents from going through the same situation. They set up a website illustrating the dangers of TWD and arranged for the wreckage of Heather's car to be exhibited at local high schools. "I was angry that she was texting and driving, and I see so many people doing it," said Heather's mother, Wendy Lerch. "I want to get her car out there and say, 'This could happen to you.'"[43]

Unfortunately, not everyone got the message the Lerches were trying to send. In an eerie coincidence, another young Rochester woman crossed the center line of a highway while texting and crashed head-on into a large truck almost exactly a year after Heather's death. She also died instantly.

"Rochester could almost be Anywhere, USA," said a report on Seattle's KING-TV following the second death. "Two women. Their lives seemingly yet to unfold. But the strikingly similar police photos of their mangled cars shatter that notion. Rochester is not just Anywhere, USA today. More than ever, it serves as a powerful example of why people should never text while driving."[44]

The Wrong Way to Sell Merchandise?

A different type of inappropriate social media usage occurred in early February 2011, during the height of the demonstrations in Egypt. Famed fashion designer Kenneth Cole Tweeted, "Millions are in an uproar in Cairo. Rumor is they heard our new spring collection is now available online."[45]

Thousands of people immediately accused Cole of taking advantage of the sacrifices and deaths of other people to sell merchandise. A few even urged a boycott of Cole products. Cole, who has a history of using current news in promotions for his company, removed the original Tweet within four hours and replaced it with another Tweet that contained an apology.

For some people, that was not enough. They put up a fake Twitter feed that linked Cole products with Nazi Germany, waterboarding torture, the floods in New Orleans and serial killer Jeffrey Dahmer, who cannibalized his victims. Cole used Facebook to issue another apology: "I apologize to everyone who was offended by my insensitive Tweet about the situation in Egypt. I've dedicated my life to raising awareness about serious social issues, and in hindsight my attempt at humor regarding a nation liberating themselves against oppression was poorly timed and absolutely inappropriate."[46]

Online Revenge

Yet another form of inappropriate communication—at least to those who are negatively impacted—arises because many personal relationships end every year. Until recently, except in very high profile cases such as movie stars or pop singers, only a handful of people outside of the unhappy couple were aware of the circumstances. The rise of online communication has changed that dynamic. People hurt by the end of a relationship often do not suffer in silence. Rather they take revenge online in blogs and websites such as DontDateHimGirl.com, which claims to have records of more than 46,000 men whose exes believe dealt with them unfairly. Sometimes the results are humorous. More often they can cause acute embarrassment, and in a few cases result in the commission of a crime.

The majority of such sites have been set up by women. Some of them exist primarily as a form of therapy, allowing women who have been dumped to gain sympathy from other women in similar circumstances. Others take a more aggressive approach, often posting photos of men and listing their supposed faults in an effort to keep other women from dating them.

Not everyone finds this trend enjoyable or even appealing. A prominent woman in New York posted a harsh video severely criticizing her soon-to-be-ex-husband that attracted nationwide attention and led to

A woman in New Hampshire sends a text message while driving. Distractions such as texting and talking on cell phones contribute to more than one-fourth of all automobile accidents.

Not Taking One for the Team?

In a National Football League playoff game in 2011, Chicago Bears quarterback Jay Cutler suffered a knee injury and went to the sideline. Without knowing anything about the severity of his injury, several players on other teams who were watching on television ripped into him via Twitter within moments after it became apparent that he would not be returning to action. "Cmon cutler u have to come back. This is the NFC championship if u didn't know," said one player. Another called him a sissy. A third said that he had had numerous knee injuries in his career and still continued to play. A fourth even said Cutler had shamed himself so badly that he did not deserve to shower with his teammates.

Fans inside the stadium and watching on television soon became aware of the virtual commotion. A new Twitter account, @JayCutlersHeart, with many Tweets questioning his courage, was launched. It did not matter that the team doctor, his coach, and many of his teammates stood up for him in the post-game news conference. The first perception of a person or an event is often the one that lingers longest. Jay Cutler had been branded as a quitter.

Quoted in Dan Wetzel, "Unprecedented Social Media Attack Dooms Cutler," Yahoo! Sports, January 24, 2011. http://sports.yahoo.com.

what some people called the first YouTube divorce. Soon afterward, Mary Elizabeth Williams of *Salon* magazine wrote, "It makes me ill to think that she represents a future in which bitter exes scream and break plates on the Internet while the rest of us sip our morning coffee, watching on the screen."[47]

Sometimes online revenge is not spurred by romantic disappointment. Take the case of a (presumably) underage teenager who stashed a dozen bottles of beer in his bedroom. His sister ratted him out to their very strict parents, who grounded him for three months. The brother conducted what he termed a "treasure hunt" in his sister's room. He found a sheet of paper entitled "My hook up list," which included the names of 10 boys and her romantic intentions with each one. A few of the names had already been tagged with "mission accomplished."

He posted the sheet on Facebook and received nearly 20 responses within an hour. Most were from boys who seemed to think it was funny. At least one of the respondents had been included on the list. He vowed to avoid the sister from then on. The sister was furious and demanded that her brother take down the posting. He told her that she had no leverage. He could simply show the list to their parents. Eventually the brother did remove the sheet, but by then the damage had been done.

To counter these and other dangers, experts encourage social media users to exercise a high degree of awareness and to safeguard personal information. Often people are who they claim they are. Sometimes they are not. A healthy skepticism may be the best approach.

Chapter Four

Reweaving the Social Fabric

The sudden rise of social media is radically altering the ways in which people have interacted for centuries, if not millennia. Many of the changes are beneficial. Others may not be.

When Texting Replaces Conversation

Some commentators suggest that social media, rather than promoting positive interactive connections, is actually helping to develop a cyberculture in which technology replaces genuine emotion. Life online becomes more important to some people than what they term "RL," or real life. As social critic and sociology professor Sherry Turkle points out in *Alone Together*, a book published in 2011 that attracted a great deal of attention, "Digital connections . . . may offer the illusion of companionship without the demands of friendship. Our networked life allows us to hide from each other, even as we are tethered to each other. We'd rather text than talk."[48]

Many people agree with Turkle. For example, communications professor Nancy Baym notes, "[Psychologist] Kenneth Gergen describes us as struggling with the 'challenge of absent presence.'. . . We may be physically present in one space, yet mentally and emotionally engaged elsewhere."[49] In other words, we may be sitting next to another person, perhaps even having a face-to-face conversation, yet our primary focus may be on a digital conversation on our computer or cell phone.

Pulitzer prize–winning editorial cartoonist David Horsey skewers "absent presence" in a cartoon titled "Texting: The Great American Distraction." The first three panels show a close-up of a boy tapping away on his cell phone. Earplugs connected to the phone ensure his complete attention to his texting. In the fourth panel he continues to type but his eyes widen. "Huh?" he asks himself. The final panel widens to show his entire family sitting at the dinner table, all absorbed in their cell phones. "Mom, why'd you text me to pass the peas?" the boy asks. "Because I couldn't get your father's attention,"[50] she replies.

Increased Communication

Not everyone agrees with this assessment. As a new form of communication, social media is still in the process of evolution, still working out the best way in which it can be used. Critics may also be looking at a somewhat mythical "golden age" of communication that never really existed in real life. In the era before Horsey's family ate dinner while texting on their cell phones, they may have had their noses buried in books or perhaps simply eaten in silence.

A family dinner is clearly not the priority for this young man. Some experts warn that online social media, easily accessed on cell phones and other mobile devices, have taken the place of direct conversation and interaction.

Kent State University education professor William Kist replies directly to Turkle: "When you go into a coffee shop and everyone is silent on their laptop, I understand what [Turkle] is saying about not talking to one another. But it is still communicating. I disagree with her. I don't see it as so black and white."[51] Indeed, there is evidence that e-mail and social networking have actually increased communication, especially for those who would otherwise have difficulty interacting due to distance or other factors.

> **"We'd rather text than talk."**[48]
>
> — Social critic and sociology professor Sherry Turkle.

And American poet James Russell Lowell may have anticipated one of digital communication's greatest possibilities in 1871 when he wrote, "The newspapers and telegraph gather the whole nation into a vast town-meeting, where everyone hears the affairs of the country discussed and where better judgment is pretty sure to make itself valid at last."[52] Substitute "Internet" for "newspapers and telegraph" and the result expresses the great hope of social networking.

Genuine Face Time

There is, however, some evidence that face-to-face contact is more advantageous than social media in promoting genuine communication. A recent book, Edward Glaeser's *Triumph of the City*, points out the benefits of people literally rubbing up against each other in urban areas to promote the development of ideas and nurture meaningful relationships. Commenting on the book, *New York Times* columnist David Brooks points out that "humans communicate best when they are physically brought together. Two University of Michigan researchers brought groups of people together face to face and asked them to play a difficult cooperation game. Then they organized other groups and had them communicate electronically. The face-to-face groups thrived. The electronic groups fractured and struggled."[53]

There is also evidence that strong, personal friendships based on longtime contact make people more willing to engage in actions leading to social change. To many observers, the success of Facebook groups such as Oscar Morales's "One Million Voices Against FARC" and Wael

Do Social Media Make Us More Isolated?

A widely circulated 2006 study reported that Americans had become increasingly more isolated for at least two decades. They were less involved in their neighborhoods and had fewer close friends in whom they could confide. The study suggested that social media played a significant role by weakening social ties. Three years later, the Pew Research Center addressed this issue in a study called "Social Isolation and New Technology."

The center confirmed that Americans do appear to be more isolated socially and that "the implications of this trend for individuals and for American society are starkly negative. However," the study authors continue, "we believe we have ruled out one likely source: new information and communication technologies such as the internet and mobile phone. Our survey finds the opposite trend amongst internet and mobile phone users; they have larger and more diverse core networks." What, then, might be the cause of this isolation? "We don't know," the authors confess.

Keith Hampton, Lauren Sessions, Eun Ja Her, and Lee Rainie, "Social Isolation and New Technology," Pew Internet & American Life Project, November 4, 2009. www.pewinternet.org.

Ghonim's "We Are All Khalid Said" are somewhat of an anomaly. As media studies professor Siva Vaidhyanthan says, "Instead of organizing, lobbying, and campaigning for better rules and regulations to ensure safe toys and cars for people everywhere, we rely on expressions of disgruntlement as a weak proxy for political action. Starting or joining a Facebook protest group suffices for many as political action."[54] Often the actual political action in such groups is minimal. "Saving the Children of Africa," a Facebook group with a membership of more than 1.7 million, raised just $12,000 for its cause—an average of $1/100$ of a penny per person.

Addicted to the Internet?

Also related to the rise of a dehumanized cyberculture is the possibility of addiction to online interaction. It is not uncommon for people to spend so many hours online that they lose interest in the world around them.

A recent study by University of Maryland's International Center for Media & the Public Agenda gives credence to this belief. During the study, more than 1,000 college students in 10 countries were asked to abstain from any use of social media for 24 hours. Virtually all reported some form of distress, and as many as one-fourth—depending on the country—could not complete the term of the study. A number described their feelings in terms of addiction. "Media is my drug; without it I was lost," said a student from the United Kingdom. "I am an addict. How could I survive 24 hours without it?"[55] An American added, "I was itching, like a crackhead, because I could not use my phone."[56]

A great deal of anecdotal evidence supports this contention. For example, an author with an impending book deadline felt overwhelmed by his need to stay connected. He went to a remote cabin to escape from his self-imposed pressure and finish his book without distractions. He could not go completely cold turkey, though. He brought his cell phone with him. He locked it in the trunk of his car, intending to check it just once a day. His plan did not work. "I kept walking out of the house to open the trunk and check the phone," he said. "I felt like an addict, like the people at work who huddle around the outdoor smoking places they keep on campus, the outdoor ashtray places. I kept going to that trunk."[57]

Clearly, people can become so absorbed in social media that they lose track of what is happening in the world around them, a situation often linked to addiction. In 2011 a mother received a 10-year prison term after her 13-month-old son accidentally drowned in a bathtub while she was playing a Facebook game. The sentencing judge rejected community service or probation, telling her, "You left this little boy in a bathtub so you could entertain yourself on the computer by playing games. And you left that 13-month-old human being, little Joseph, incredibly, for those reasons."[58]

Addiction—or Passion?

Not everyone agrees that the Internet and social media are addictive, at least not in the clinical sense. Responding to requests from some of its members, in 2007 the American Medical Association voted to add Internet Addiction Disorder (IAD) to the next edition of the *Diagnostic and Statistical Manual of Mental Disorders*. In this view, IAD is compulsive use of the Internet—such as computer games, social networking, Internet shopping, and similar behaviors—that interferes with normal daily life. But the AMA quickly backtracked from its original vote and said that the issue needed more study. "There is nothing here to suggest that this is a complex physiological disease state akin to alcoholism or other

The American Academy of Pediatrics notes that kids with already low self-esteem can experience further hurt when they see friends and classmates with many Facebook "friends" and many exciting-sounding activities that they do not have or cannot take part in.

substance abuse disorders, and it doesn't get to have the word addiction attached to it,"[59] said Stuart Gitlow, an expert in the field of addiction.

Turkle suggests that computer users may be getting a bum rap, falling victim to what is almost guilt by association. She notes that "the computer's holding power is a phenomenon frequently referred to in terms associated with drug addiction. It is striking that the word 'user' is associated mainly with computers and drugs."[60]

New York Times lifestyle columnist Virginia Heffernan goes even further. She believes that there may be a certain amount of social snobbery connected with the whole concept of addiction. She wryly notes that "in general, if a pastime is not classy, those who love it are 'addicted.' Opera and poetry buffs are 'passionate.'"[61] In particular, she cites a young woman named Gabriela, who worries that she may be addicted. Gabriela spends several hours a day on a variety of social media—sometimes staying up well past midnight—and even sleeps with her laptop so she can listen to music she has downloaded. Heffernan sees no cause for concern. "No student who's making decent grades needs to get off the Internet just because it would look more respectable or comprehensible to be playing chess, throwing a Frisbee or reading a George Orwell paperback. The Internet as Gabriela uses it simply is intellectual life, and play."[62]

> **"No student who's making decent grades needs to get off the Internet just because it would look more respectable or comprehensible to be playing chess, throwing a Frisbee or reading a George Orwell paperback."[62]**
>
> — *New York Times* columnist Virginia Heffernan.

Facebook Depression

Another unintended consequence of the rise of social media is so-called "Facebook depression." A 2011 study by the American Academy of Pediatrics acknowledged the increasingly pervasive role of social media and noted that kids already suffering with low self-esteem can become even worse when they see that friends and classmates have more Facebook friends and more enjoyable activities than they do. Lack of response to posts and friend requests makes the situation worse. "Kids can be insecure in general, so when you take a kid that is having trouble with peers and having trouble to begin with, Facebook can heighten those anxieties to a huge degree,"[63] says study author Gwenn Schurgin O'Keeffe.

The malady is not limited to teenagers. Another 2011 study, conducted by Stanford University, shows virtually the same feelings among college students, who often get an unrealistic picture of the lives of their online friends. Psychologist David Swanson, one of the principal researchers, says, "What you put on display is how great your life is—the cars you drive, the vacations you go on. Nobody's life is that perfect and so, whenever you start to compare your life to those images, you're going to be depressed, because you're going to feel like your life is lacking."[64] Swanson's point is that most people have little or no face-to-face contact with their online friends. This type of contact would reveal that those friends have their own ups and downs and that their postings simply reflect the highlights of their lives. They keep their doubts and disappointments to themselves.

Adults are also susceptible. For example, the well-publicized joy of pregnant women may make their infertile friends feel inferior. These and similar feelings obviously can occur without social media, but social media's all-pervasive influence helps to worsen the situation by providing continual visual images.

A Place to Find Support

Sometimes depression, whether Facebook-induced or otherwise, can take extreme form and provide fodder for those who maintain that Facebook friends are not as genuine as real, flesh-and-blood ones. There are many episodes of people in effect crying out for help on Facebook and other social media but receiving caustic feedback from their "friends"—which in extreme cases leads to suicide.

On the other hand, a 2011 study by University of Wisconsin researchers suggests that Facebook may serve not only as a means of discovering depression but also of providing assistance with its symptoms. About 25 percent of the study group posted one or more symptoms of depression. When they did, their friends rallied around them. "People are getting support from other Facebook users when they display these comments, so it may be used as a mini-support group for depression," says Megan Moreno, a lead author of the study. "Given the frequency of depression symptoms displayed, it's possible that depression disclosures on Facebook may actually help to reduce the stigma around mental illness."[65] The researchers also emphasize that while no one should use Facebook as an actual diagnostic tool or method of treatment, it may be useful in identifying people who are considering suicide and thereby allow early intervention.

FOMO and Its Discontents

Somewhat similar to Facebook depression is FOMO, or fear of missing out. According to journalist Jenna Wortham, FOMO "refers to the blend of anxiety, inadequacy and irritation that can flare up while skimming social media like Facebook, Twitter, Foursquare and Instagram. Billions of Twitter messages, status updates and photographs provide thrilling glimpses of the daily lives and activities of friends, 'frenemies,' co-workers and peers."[66]

For example, a person might be perfectly content sitting home alone one evening and watching television, until online updates reveal that one group of friends is going to a movie and another group is attending a concert. Suddenly the person begins to fear that he or she has made the wrong decision about the best way of spending the evening. It may not matter that this person has had a tough week at work and could use some down time to recharge mental and physical batteries.

FOMO is nothing new. People have always been aware of what their friends are doing without them. The difference today is that these reminders come in real time. Seeing the smiling faces of friends as they mill about in the midst of hundreds of other happy concertgoers makes it obvious what a person is missing by having chosen to not attend. It is more immediate and meaningful than talking to one of them the day afterward, and frequently leads to regretting the decision not to participate.

Anonymous Expressions of Hatred

One clear downside to social media is the cloak of anonymity it often extends, which allows people to express harsh and vulgar opinions they would not dare say openly. It offers a forum for high-tech sociopaths to "express" their bile and hatred without fear of retribution.

Getting Treatment

Whether Internet addictive disorder (IAD) is a "real" medical condition or not, some people are willing to treat it as if it is. The Heavensfield Retreat Center in Fall City, Washington, recently launched its reSTART Internet Addiction Recovery Program, which focuses on perceived addictions to gaming, the Internet, and cell phones. The program consists of a variety of activities such as individual and group counseling, outdoor recreational opportunities, improving fitness and overall health, and 12-step meetings similar to those used by Alcoholics Anonymous and similar organizations. It lasts for 45 days and costs $14,500.

While detractors say that the cost is too high, program officials maintain that it is actually less than comparable 30-day inpatient programs for alcoholism. As journalist Jacqui Cheng points out, "With some people trying to use IAD as an excuse for poor work performance, reSTART and other programs like it may eventually become as commonplace as drug and alcohol counseling."

Jacqui Cheng, "Addicted to the Internet? $14,500, Please, at First US Rehab," Ars Technica, August 2009. http://arstechnica.com.

While anonymous attacks are nothing new, the vast reach of the Internet gives these opinions considerably more exposure. When Massachusetts senator Scott Brown appeared on the TV program *60 Minutes* and discussed his childhood sexual molestation by a camp counselor, many people attacked him on the show's website. And the sexual assault by a mob on journalist Lara Logan while she was covering the protests in Egypt unleashed a torrent of abuse. In both cases nearly all of the nasty commentators hid behind aliases that gave no clue to their actual identity.

Sometimes expressions of bigotry and intolerance emerge even when users are clearly identified. In March 2011, a coed at the University of California at Los Angeles (UCLA) posted a three-minute YouTube video in the wake of the earthquake and tsunami that devastated Japan. In the video, she took issue with the frantic efforts of Japanese students at UCLA to contact their families, saying that they should act more like Americans. The rant went viral.

The university declined to discipline the coed, saying that to do so would violate her right to free speech and that she was not threatening anyone. By then another form of "discipline" had emerged. A few days after posting the video, the coed announced that she was leaving school, saying that her family had been continually harassed and that she had even received death threats—many of them posted anonymously online.

Dumbing Down—or Wising Up

Critics such as Nicholas Carr maintain that social networking and other Internet activities represent a "dumbing down" of society, that people are no longer able to focus on activities requiring more thought and commitment such as reading books and engaging in lengthy conversation. Carr went so far as to suggest that his brain was actually being altered by his online experiences. In his view, quiet and contemplation are essential ingredients in creating genuine empathy, conditions that constant updates on Facebook and a steady barrage of e-mails and text messages do not permit.

English professor and social critic Mark Bauerlein says something similar in his book *The Dumbest Generation: How the Digital Age Stupifies Young Americans and Jeopardizes Our Future*. He calls contemporary teens a "portrait of vigorous, indiscriminate ignorance."[67] One time Bauerlein told an audience of college students that they were much more likely to know the identity of *American Idol* contestants than the name of the Speaker of the House of Representatives. Someone yelled back that *American Idol* was more important—thereby helping to make his point.

Yet contrary to such fears, there is evidence that social media users are becoming more sophisticated and more socially aware. Management professor Don Tapscott conducted a two-year, $4 million study of what he calls the Net Generation. Born in the mid-to-late 1980s and early 1990s, "[the Net Generation] were different from any other generation because they were the first to grow up surrounded by digital media. . . . For the first time in history, children are more comfortable, knowledgeable and literate than their parents with an innovation central to society."[68]

Tapscott's findings made him very optimistic in spite of the negative comments from people such as Carr and Bauerlein. "As the first global generation ever, the Net Geners are smarter, quicker, and more tolerant of diversity than their predecessors," he writes. "With their reflexes tuned to speed and freedom, these empowered young people are beginning to transform every institution of modern life."[69]

No Strangers to Controversy

As the dispute about "dumbing down" suggests, there is no consensus on the long-term effects of social media on people's ability to relate to each other. It may, however, be worth noting that controversies over the introduction of new technology and new ways of behavior have a long history. In 1797 a pamphlet called *Novel Reading, a Cause of Female Depravity* railed against literacy for girls. Nineteenth-century Luddites and their predecessors objected—sometimes violently—to the introduction of the means of mass production in England. In 1956 Minister Albert Carter said, "The effect of rock and roll on young people, is to turn them into devil worshippers; to stimulate self expression through sex; to provoke lawlessness. . . . It is an evil influence on the youth of our country."[70]

> "As the first global generation ever, the Net Geners are smarter, quicker, and more tolerant of diversity than their predecessors."[69]
>
> — Management professor Don Tapscott.

And nearly 2,500 years ago, the Greek philosopher Socrates railed against the introduction of the alphabet and its supposedly negative effect on the Greek oral tradition of literature:

This discovery of yours will create forgetfulness in the learners' souls, because they will not use their memories; they will trust to the external written characters and not remember of themselves. The specific which you have discovered is an aid not to memory, but to reminiscence, and you give your disciples not truth, but only the semblance of truth; they will be hearers of many things and will have learned nothing: they will appear to be omniscient and will generally know nothing: they will be tiresome company, having the show of wisdom without the reality.[71]

The ancient Greek philosopher Socrates (pictured) worried that the introduction of the alphabet would destroy thought and wisdom. This dire scenario did not come to pass, offering support to those who say that online communication and social networking will not lead to humanity's ruin either.

Yet none of these fears came to pass. Female literacy has produced millions of talented women who have contributed immeasurably to society. Mass production has raised the overall standard of living. Teens who listened to rock 'n' roll did not succumb to devil worship. And the alphabet has provided for the publication of countless millions of books and magazines—as well as making it possible to communicate online. So it seems that the odds may be in favor of a similar positive outcome for social media.

Chapter Five

The Future of Online Social Media

What lies ahead for social media? Prediction is an inexact science. For example, in 1943 then–IBM president Thomas Watson showed little faith in the future of computers when he said, "I think there is a world market for maybe five computers."[72] Ironically, several decades later IBM developed the first successful personal computer, the predecessor of the computers now found in many American homes. On the other hand, science fiction writers have a tradition of creating worlds that years later bear remarkable resemblance to real life. This happened with French author Jules Verne, whose 1863 novel *Paris in the Twentieth Century* describes such things as glass skyscrapers, television sets, automobiles that run on gasoline, pocket calculators—and a worldwide telegraphic network for instant communication, a fictional forerunner of today's Internet.

A 1994 video clip featuring then–*Today* show hosts Bryant Gumbel and Katie Couric began making the rounds of YouTube early in 2011. It helps to show how far online communication has come in just a few years, as well as what may lie ahead. The clip begins with Gumbel expressing mystification about the meaning of the @ symbol. Then he asks,

"What is Internet anyway?"

"Internet is that massive computer network, the one that's becoming really big now," Couric replies.

Almost irritably, Gumbel says, "What do you mean? What do you do, write to it, like mail?"

"No," Couric answers. "A lot of people use it to communicate." Then she asks the production crew off-camera if any of them know what it is.

"A giant computer network," comes the response. "It's getting bigger and bigger all the time."[73]

A Constantly Changing Picture

If anything, "bigger and bigger all the time" understates the astounding technological leaps of the last few years. The rate of change and growth has been breathtakingly swift since that *Today* show, and this torrid pace is likely to continue.

The Internet and online communication have come a long way in a little over two decades. **Today** *show hosts Katie Couric and Bryant Gumbel, pictured in 1994, knew little about the Internet in those days as is clear from an on-air conversation in which they puzzled over exactly what the Internet is.*

With changes coming so rapidly, companies are likely to see changes in where they stand in the marketplace. In the arena of online communication and social media, it can be tough to stay on top. Less than two decades ago, Compuserve was the major provider of e-mail. It was soon brushed aside by America Online (AOL), which is little more than a niche service today. So the dominance of current giants such as Facebook and Twitter—which themselves have been in existence for just a few years—may be challenged by new companies that are either in the fledgling stage or that have not even been created yet.

Google is taking a page from Facebook and adding a "+1" button as a way of recommending search results and ads. Click-

> **"What is Internet anyway?"** [73]
>
> — Former *Today* host Bryant Gumbel.

ing on it will function in a way similar to Facebook's "Like" button and may represent a first step toward making Google more social. If your friends like a certain site, Google reasons, you are likely to as well.

The Development of Niche Networks

One trend is that social media will become more and more targeted, giving rise to numerous niche networks based on common interests and activities. Already a number of new companies have sprung up, having just a fraction of the membership of the giants but apparently filling a need. These new companies are likely to experience steady growth without challenging the overall supremacy of the far larger companies.

For example, a California woman recently wanted to share a photo of her garden. Rather than using Facebook, she posted it on Path, a new network that caps the number of friends at 50. As she explains, "The people I have on my Path are the people who are going to care about the day-to-day random events in my life, or if my dog does something funny. On Facebook, I have colleagues or family members who wouldn't necessarily be interested in those things—and also that I wouldn't necessarily want to have view those things."[74] In just a short period of time, Path has attracted hundreds of thousands of users by emphasizing the difference between acquaintances and genuine friends and allowing its users to focus on the latter group.

Shizzlr, another new company, launched by two University of Connecticut business students, came about because its organizers were frustrated with the difficulties of making plans on Facebook. "You put out a status about weekend plans and, all of a sudden, you get your uncle commenting that he wants to go hiking with you and your friends,"[75] says coorganizer Nick Jaensch. To keep uncles and others from trying to horn into situations where they are not really wanted, Shizzlr groups are capped at 20. "Facebook is for every person you've met or have come across," Jaensch adds. "Shizzlr is for your actual 20 friends and the people you hang out with. . . . Everybody is involved in a group message, everyone is up-to-date and everyone can give their input."[76]

Facebook has methods of limiting the amount of information sent to friends, but many users find these methods hard to understand. So in 2010 the company introduced Groups, which establishes smaller, more tightly organized sets of specially selected friends. In just a few months, the company says that 50 million of these smaller groups, with a median average size of just eight people, were established. "We realized there wasn't a way to share with these groups of people that were already established in your real life—family, book club members, a sports team," says Peter Deng, director of product for Facebook Groups. "It's one of the fastest-growing products within Facebook. Usage has been pretty phenomenal."[77] Google is also jumping on the minigroup bandwagon, releasing a cell phone app for texting with a small group of close friends.

Breaking Bread Together

Another approach to small-scale social networking is illustrated by Grubwithus, a startup that attracted more than 10,000 members in less than a year after its launch in August 2010. Grubwithus combines social networking and old-fashioned dinner parties. Members peruse a list of meals in their city, sign up for the one they want, then provide some basic information about themselves that is shared online with their soon-to-be fellow diners. The founders of Grubwithus see it as a way of expanding their members' friendship network in a comfortable, nonthreatening environment.

"Online contact and networking might replace offline interactions, but offline is still so precious that we're creating ways to bring offline even more front and center," says S. Shyam Sundar of Penn State University's

A "Soul" for the Web

Another recent mobile phone app reveals the virtually limitless possibilities for mobile phones that are likely to be developed in upcoming years. In 2010, according to *New York Times* columnist Maureen Dowd, "Pope Benedict XVI urged priests to help people see the face of Christ on the Web, through blogs, Web sites and videos; priests could give the Web a 'soul,' he said, by preaching theology through new technology." Three Catholic computer programmers quickly responded to the pope's request by developing "Confession: A Roman Catholic App." It guides users through the Ten Commandments with age- and sex-related questions to help them focus on their sins. In effect, it creates a kind of "cheat sheet" to carry into the confessional. Children, for example, may be asked if they have used swear words, while teens might be quizzed about bullying. After going to confession—a priest must still give absolution— the user's slate is literally wiped clean. Father Dan Scheidt, who helped in the app's creation, said, "Human relations are shifting more and more to being mediated by some of these gadgets. If this is the bridge for people to have a more meaningful encounter about what's deepest in their heart, I think it's going to serve the good."

Maureen Dowd, "Forgive Me Father, for I Have Linked," *New York Times*, February 8, 2011. www.nytimes.com.

Media Effects Research Lab, in explaining the appeal of such groups and why they are likely to proliterate in the future. "We're using social technology to feed our need to meet up and close the gap between all the social networking that we do from a distance."[78] It seems certain that other companies will follow this pattern.

Acting as Filters

Social media are likely to take on more importance as filters in areas such as job searches. Many companies now require prospective employees to take personality tests. A 2011 study by University of Maryland research-ers suggests that an analysis of Facebook pages can give almost the same information without the time and expense of formal tests.

The researchers examined the public profiles of nearly 300 Facebook users, paying particular attention to things such as membership in or-ganizations, favorite activities, and prefer-ences in TV shows and movies. Then the users took a standard test measuring the so-called big five personality traits: agree-ableness, conscientiousness, extroversion, neuroticism, and openness to experience. "It turns out you can get to within 10 percent of a person's personality score by looking at Facebook," according to Jennifer Golbeck, a computer sci-ence professor and codirector of the Human-Computer Interaction Lab at Maryland, one of the leading figures in the study. "If we can better understand people's relationships with one another, who they will trust online, potentially we can understand who they should interact with. . . . Huge professional or personal decisions are based on what other people are like."[79]

> "You can get to within 10 percent of a person's personality score by looking at Facebook."[79]
>
> — Computer science professor Jennifer Golbeck.

Golbeck is not through with social media studies. She and her col-leagues plan on using similar methodology when they examine the way in which people Tweet each other. The knowledge that these and similar studies reveal can help companies make better hiring decisions by identifying people who are more likely to fit in with their current employees.

College admissions are another area in which Facebook and Twitter are likely to play increasingly important roles. As budget cuts force colleges and universities to become more selective, social networks can provide additional clues about applicants. According to a recent survey conducted by the National Association for Col-lege Admission Counseling, as many as one-fourth of colleges use Facebook and search engines such as Google to provide "sources of additional information for critical decision making. No longer can students place damaging material online without potential conse-quences."[80]

Social Media in Motion

Because people spend so much of their time in their cars, automobile manufacturers are trying to equip their products with online accessibility. Toyota will introduce its own private social networking site, Toyota Friend, in Japan in 2012 and eventually expand the service worldwide. Initially the site will focus on electric and hybrid cars, providing updates similar to Twitter regarding things such as the car's battery level and the location of nearby charging stations. Exchanges can be kept quiet or shared with other Toyota Friends users. Toyota eventually plans on extending the service to include social media sites such as Facebook and Twitter.

Another hint of the automobile social networking future came during the 2011 Super Bowl with an ad for the Chevrolet Cruze. The ad begins with the last moments of a date between two young adults. The man gets in his car, checks his Facebook status and breaks out in a big

A Toyota executive introduces the company's private social networking site, Toyota Friend. The Japanese car maker hopes to communicate with Toyota owners around the world via Twitter-like messages and other features offered on various social networking sites.

smile when he hears that the woman has updated her status to "the best first date—ever!" Allowing such real-time Facebook updates is a new feature of General Motors' OnStar technology, and company representatives suggest that the feature will become increasingly interactive.

The Internet in the Legal Arena

The proliferation of more and more forms of social media will likely result in the passage of new regulations and laws. The Food and Drug Administration (FDA), for example, is likely to seek regulations about Internet sales of medical products. Such regulations could have a particular effect on Twitter because of its 140-character limit. That is not nearly enough to fully describe drugs, their dosages, potential side effects, and other information consumers need to know. The Federal Trade Commission (FTC) is trying to regulate Internet business practices. In 2010 Senator Charles Schumer called on the FTC to establish privacy guidelines. "I am asking the FTC to use the authority given to it to examine practices in the disclosure of private information from social networking sites and to ensure users have the ability to prohibit the sharing of personal information,"[81] he said. However, many people oppose government regulations, and their enactment will depend largely on the party affiliation of future presidents and the US Congress.

The rapid pace of social media expansion—along with its abuses—means that the legal system is often playing catch-up. In 1998 the US Congress passed the Children's Online Privacy and Protection Act (COP-PA), which places substantial limitations on the ability of children under 13 being able to participate in social media, especially those that seek personal information.

More recently, state and local jurisdictions have been scrambling to deal with the many issues that have arisen. As of the beginning of 2011, for example, 34 states had enacted laws dealing specifically with cyberbullying. The likelihood is that many—if not all—of the remaining 16 will follow suit. At least in part because of free speech issues, sexting appears to be a special case. While adults who sext with teens may still be charged with felonies, recent trends indicate that penalties for teens themselves may actually lessen, from felonies to a range of misdemeanors.

When it comes to actual law enforcement, a new development is the increasing willingness of police departments to establish Twitter

Twitter Posses?

An incident in May 2011 illustrates another aspect of Twitter's potential role in law enforcement. Canadian web analyst Sean Power's MacBook was stolen while he was visiting New York, but when he returned home Power was able to track it through a software program he had installed. The program gave him a good look at the thief—and much more.

"Not only did I have his face, but I also had a screen shot of what the person was doing," Power said. "I even had his bank account with the total amount of money that he had."

Power reported the situation to police, even providing the location of the bar where the thief was using his MacBook. But the police said they could not take action until Power filed a report.

Twitter users were not so hesitant. Many Tweeted suggestions for dealing with the situation. Two went further. Despite Power's objections, they went to the bar and confronted the thief, who quickly surrendered the laptop. Power did not press charges, so the thief was not arrested.

In this case, the situation ended peacefully. But similar situations could be different in the future if Twitter users decide to take the law into their own hands. "It's super, super dangerous," Power said.

CBC News, "Twitter Posse Helps Ottawa Man Recover Laptop," May 13, 2001. www.cbc.ca.

accounts. For example, police could notify the public about traffic problems caused by large-scale events such as concerts and athletic events and suggest alternate routes. It could also be an effective way of alerting the public to emergency situations. And it may also facilitate two-way communication between the public and police.

Moves Involving Mobile Phones

In addition to changes in usage and regulation, the ways in which people access the means of social networking and communication will also undergo significant changes. One of these changes is already well established, and that is a dramatic rise in the use of mobile phones to facilitate connectivity. This rise is especially notable in developing countries where much of the population exists on a few dollars a day and where access to fast Internet computer service is lacking—let alone the ready availability of computers themselves. This trend should continue into the foreseeable future and bring increasing millions of people into the social media sphere of influence.

One result is the creation of more and more cell phone applications. For example, motorists burn billions of gallons of gas circling congested downtown areas as they seek parking places, vastly increasing traffic congestion and endangering pedestrians. In spring 2011 the city of San Francisco introduced a program called SF Park that inserts wireless sensors on nearly 20,000 metered parking spaces and slots in parking garages to indicate when they are no longer occupied. This information is transferred to the application within a minute, making nearby drivers aware of the now-available space.

To further refine the system, officials hope to program parking meters and garage spaces remotely, raising prices in areas already heavily trafficked and lowering the cost in more remote locations—and add this information to displays of available spots. This will help equalize traffic flow.

Los Angeles has plans for a similar project, called Downtown LA ExpressPark Project. Officials are keenly aware of the scrutiny their programs will attract. Los Angeles Department of Transportation senior engineer Dan Mitchell notes, "I think many cities are watching San Francisco and Los Angeles to see how this experiment works."[82]

Thin Clients

The rise of cell phones illustrates another aspect of social media that will carry over to the future. For many people, the demand for applications directly available through the Internet far outpaces computer-linked software programs such as word processing. Technology author Nicholas Carr believes that these apps, as well as virtually everything else that a traditional personal computer does, can be accessed through a "thin client," a single terminal that somewhat resembles a monitor directly linked to the Internet. Thin clients are far cheaper than PCs, making them much more appealing to cash-strapped individuals and countries. They also eliminate thick software instruction manuals frequently written in almost impenetrable prose, the need to frequently upgrade software, and the necessity of virus protection. The upshot, according to Carr, is that "we may find, twenty or so years from now, that the personal computer has become a museum piece, a reminder of a curious time when all of us were forced to be amateur computer technicians."[83]

One of the primary reasons for developments such as these is Moore's Law, a remarkably accurate observation that Intel chip manufacturer cofounder Gordon Moore first made in 1965. According to this "law," computer power doubles about every two years. At the same time, computer chips get smaller and less expensive to produce. Just as today people assume that walls of rooms are wired and all we need to get light and power is to flip a switch, in the not-too-distant future we will assume that these walls are also wired for the Internet, and we will look for the Internet portal.

Michio Kaku predicts even greater advances as a result of Moore's Law. "Today, we can communicate with the Internet via our computers and cell phones," he observes. "But in the future, the Internet will be everywhere—in wall screens, furniture, on billboards, and even in our glasses and contact lenses. When we blink, we will go online."[84]

> **"When we blink, we will go online."[84]**
>
> — Theoretical physicist Michio Kaku.

With funding from the US Army, the Flexible Display Center at Arizona State University is developing ultrathin, unbreakable screens so flexible they could be folded and put into a user's pocket. Mobile phones might contain a screen that could be unrolled until it is the size of a keyboard—only much lighter—and thereby make texting faster and much easier.

More Intriguing Possibilities

Larger screens would cover entire walls and offer a number of intriguing possibilities for online communication. One is virtual family gatherings, with images of relatives appearing on all four walls. Another is teleconferencing. A third would involve online dating services, which have become popular in recent years. Prospective daters may be able to interact with life-size images of a possible partner displayed on their living room wall. As they talk, their screen will scan that person's real history to detect any lies in their biographies—something contemporary sites cannot do.

Internet glasses offer another method of connectivity. In one form being developed at the Massachusetts Institute of Technology (MIT), a tiny lens is affixed to the corner of the frame of the glasses. A quick tap and it drops directly in front of the eye, displaying an entire computer screen. A handheld cell phone–size box allows users to control the display. The frames might also hold a tiny video camera, which could broadcast directly onto the Internet and thereby provide instant updating of the social networks to which the wearer belongs.

Connectivity Backlash?

In spite of all these and other advances in technology relating to social media, a backlash to continual connectivity may be brewing. In recent years, more and more locations—hotels, ferries, cafes, resorts and so forth—have advertised that they offer wireless Internet access, either for free or for a small fee. It is possible that in the future, the lack of Internet access may become a selling point, as people seek refuge from the continual onslaught of information and updates.

There may also be a psychological cost to continual connectivity. As Sherry Turkle notes, "These days, looking at sociable robots and digitized friends, one might assume that what we want is to be always in touch and never alone. . . . But if we pay attention to the real consequences of what we think we want, we may discover what we really want. We may want some stillness and solitude."[85]

While considerable truth doubtless lies in Turkle's observation, it is not likely to slow down the increasing reliance on social media. As the authors of another Pew study noted in 2010, "The social benefits of internet use will far outweigh the negatives over the next decade, according to experts who responded to a survey about the future of the internet. They say this is because email, social networks, and other online tools offer 'low-friction' opportunities to create, enhance, and rediscover social ties that make a difference in people's lives. The internet lowers traditional communications constraints of cost, geography, and time; and it supports the type of open information sharing that brings people together."[86]

One technology company is developing a terminal that can be directly linked to the Internet. Called a "thin client," this device would be much cheaper than personal computers and would not need lengthy software instruction manuals or frequent software upgrades.

The Wired World

This point of view finds considerable support in the wired world. A key figure in Google's rise is Amit Singhal, one of the company's key engineers. Singhal ranks in the top 50 in two magazine polls: *India Abroad*'s "50 Most Influential Indian Americans" and *Fortune*'s "The smartest people in tech." So his thoughts carry considerable weight. As he says, "Every citizen in the world can access the power of hundreds of thousands of computers. . . . The web has become an endlessly open channel where people share ideas and information. That has the power to enrich people's lives and I'm very excited about where this world is headed."[87]

At this point no one can say whether the rosy future predicted by digital utopians such as Singhal will outweigh the downside and serve to bring people closer together, as individuals and as nations. But the end result of all these developments seems likely to be an even more wired world, one in which the potential dangers of social media may never go away but in which the benefits continue to expand.

Source Notes

Introduction: Tweeting Oscar's Big Night

1. Quoted in Nicole Ferraro, "Social Media Win, Hosts & Ads Lose, During #Oscars," *Internet Evolution*, February 28, 2011. www.internetevolution.com.
2. Quoted in Jennifer Preston, "Republicans Sharpening Online Tools for 2012," *New York Times*, April 19, 2011. www.nytimes.com.

Chapter One: The Wired World

3. Aryn Baker, "How Can We Trust Them?," *Time*, May 20, 2011, p. 60.
4. Quoted in Melissa Bell, "Sohaib Athar's Tweets from the Attack on Osama bin Laden—Read Them All Below," *Washington Post*, May 2, 2011. www.washingtonpost.com.
5. Quoted in Bell, "Sohaib Athar's Tweets."
6. Quoted in "Osama bin Laden Dead: Osama's Neighbour Sohaib Athar Tweets His Way to Celebrity Status," *Economic Times*, May 3, 2011. http://articles.economictimes.indiatimes.com.
7. Quoted in David Bauder, "Where Were You When You Heard? On Social Media," *Seattle Times*, May 3, 2011. http://seattletimes.nwsource.com.
8. Quoted in Bell, "Sohaib Athar's Tweets."
9. Quoted in Bell, "Sohaib Athar's Tweets."
10. Quoted in Chris Lefkow, "Facebook Reuniting Tornado Victims with Memories," *Discovery News*, April 27, 2011. http://news.discovery.com.
11. Michio Kaku, *Physics of the Future: How Science Will Shape Human Destiny and Our Daily Lives by the Year 2100*. New York: Doubleday, 2011, p. 15.
12. David Kirkpatrick, *The Facebook Effect*. New York: Simon & Schuster, 2010, p. 7.
13. Peter Applebome, "Trespass at School. Post Prom Invitation. Get Barred from Event. Become Famous," *New York Times*, May 12, 2011. www.nytimes.com.

14. Quoted in Owen Lei, "Man Apologizes for Traffic Jam via Twitter," KING-TV, March 5, 2011. www.king5.com.
15. Jack Bell, "M.L.S. Finding New Center in the Pacific Northwest," *New York Times*, March 14, 2011. www.nytimes.com.
16. Quoted in Jack Bell, "New Center," *New York Times*.
17. Quoted in Judy Battista, "N.F.L. Labor Dispute Plays Out on Twitter," *New York Times*, February 21, 2011. www.nytimes.com.

Chapter Two: Social Networking Takes to the Streets

18. Quoted in Kirkpatrick, *The Facebook Effect*, p. 2.
19. Quoted in Juan Forero and Karin Brulliard, "Anti-FARC Rallies Held Worldwide," *Washington Post*, February 5, 2008. www.washingtonpost.com.
20. Quoted in Elizabeth Dickinson, "Chained in the Colombian Jungle, *Foreign Policy*, September 24, 2010. www.foreignpolicy.com.
21. Quoted in Jan Gerhard, "Oscar Morales on Political Engagement with Younger Generations," Total Politics, February 10, 2010. www.totalpolitics.com.
22. Quoted in Rania Abouzeid, "Bouazizi: The Man Who Set Himself and Tunisia on Fire," *Time*, January 21, 2011. www.time.com.
23. Quoted in Yasmine Ryan, "How Tunisia's Revolution Began," *Al Jazeera*, January 26, 2011. http://english.aljazeera.net.
24. Quoted in Nathan Oliverez-Giles, "Tunisia Protesters Use Facebook, Twitter and YouTube to Help Organize and Report," *Los Angeles Times*, January 14, 2011. http://latimesblogs.latimes.com.
25. Roger Cohen, "The Arab Gyre," *New York Times*, April 18, 2011. www.nytimes.com.
26. Quoted in Jack Schenker, "Mohamed ElBaradei Warns of 'Tunisia-Style Explosion' in Egypt," *Guardian* (Manchester, UK), January 18, 2011. www.guardian.co.uk.
27. Quoted in Mike Giglio, "The Facebook Freedom Fighter," *Newsweek*, February 21, 2011, p. 15.
28. Giglio, "The Facebook Freedom Fighter," p. 15.
29. Ernesto Londono, "Egyptian Man's Death Became Symbol of Callous State," *Washington Post*, February 9, 2011. www.washingtonpost.com.
30. Quoted in Londono, "Egyptian Man's Death Became Symbol of Callous State."

31. Quoted in Anthony Shadid, "Exiles Shaping World's Image of Syria Revolt," *New York Times*, April 23, 2011. www.nytimes.com.
32. Oscar Morales, "One Million Voices Against the FARC: A Milestone for Freedom," George W. Bush Presidential Center, February 4, 2011.

Chapter Three: Online Perils and Pitfalls

33. Quoted in Great-Quotes.com, June 3, 2011. www.great-quotes.com.
34. Quoted in Jan Hoffman, "A Girl's Nude Photo, and Altered Lives," *New York Times*, March 26, 2011. www.nytimes.com.
35. Quoted in Hoffman, "A Girl's Nude Photo."
36. Quoted in Hoffman, "A Girl's Nude Photo."
37. Quoted in Jessica Leshnoff, "Sexting Not Just for Kids: Adults from Many Different Backgrounds Are Now Sending and Receiving Explicit Text Messages," *AARP Magazine*, November 2009. www.aarp.org.
38. Quoted in Kathy McCabe, "Teen's Suicide Prompts a Look at Bullying," *Boston Globe*, January 24, 2010. http://mobile.boston.com.
39. Quoted in Russell Goldman, "Teens Indicted After Allegedly Taunting Girl Who Hanged Herself," ABC News, March 29, 2010. http://abcnews.go.com.
40. Quoted in Tim Arango, "Text Messages Proliferate as Threats in Iraq," *New York Times*, April 26, 2011. www.nytimes.com.
41. Quoted in Arango, "Text Messages Proliferate."
42. Quoted in Nancy Baym, *Personal Connections in the Digital Age*. Malden, MA: Polity, 2010, p. 33.
43. Quoted in Susan Gilmore, "Daughter's Death in Accident While Texting a Warning to Others," *Seattle Times*, February 19, 2011. http://seattletimes.nwsource.com.
44. Quoted in Mark Horner, "Small Town Sees Eerily Similar Fatal Texting Crashes Nearly 1 Year Apart," KING-TV, February 19, 2001. http://heathersstory.org.
45. Quoted in Leanne Italie, "Oops! Kenneth Cole Apologizes for Egypt Tweet," *Seattle Times*, February 3, 2011. http://seattletimes.nwsource.com.
46. Quoted in Italie, "Oops! Kenneth Cole Apologizes."
47. Quoted in Tracy Clark-Flory, "Romantic Revenge in the Internet Age," *Salon*, February 9, 2011. www.salon.com.

Chapter Four: Reweaving the Social Fabric

48. Sherry Turkle, *Alone Together: Why We Expect More from Technology and Less from Each Other*. New York: Basic Books, 2011, p. 1.

49. Baym, *Personal Connections in the Digital Age*, p. 3.

50. David Horsey, "Modern Life," *Seattle Post-Intelligencer*, May 9, 2011. http://blog.seattlepi.com.

51. Quoted in Paul Harris, "Social Networking Under Fresh Attack as Tide of Cyber-scepticism Sweeps US," *Guardian* (Manchester, UK), January 22, 2011. www.guardian.co.uk.

52. Quoted in Paul Grosswiler, "Historical Hopes, Media Fears, and the Electronic Town Meeting Concept: Where Technology Meets Democracy or Demagogy?," *Journal of Communication Inquiry*, April 1, 1998. www.accessmylibrary.com.

53. David Brooks, "The Splendor of Cities," *New York Times*, February 7, 2011. www.nytimes.com.

54. Siva Vaidhyanthan, *The Googlization of Everything (and Why We Should Worry)*. Berkeley, and Los Angeles: University of California Press, 2011, p. 43.

55. Quoted in International Center for Media & the Public Agenda (IC-MPA), "The World Unplugged: Going 24 Hours Without Media," University of Maryland.

56. Quoted in International Center for Media & the Public Agenda (IC-MPA), "The World Unplugged."

57. Quoted in Turkle, *Alone Together*, p. 227.

58. Quoted in "13-Month-Old Boy Drowns as Mom Plays Facebook, Receives 10 Year Prison Sentence," Associated Press, April 15, 2011. www.netaddictionrecovery.com.

59. Quoted in Eric Bangeman, "AMA Rethinks Classifying Video Game Addiction as Mental Disorder," Ars Technica, June, 2007. http://arstechnica.com.

60. Sherry Turkle, *Life on the Screen: Identity in the Age of the Internet*. New York: Simon & Schuster, 1995, p. 30.

61. Virginia Heffernan, "Miss G.: A Case of Internet Addiction," *New York Times*, April 9, 2011. http://opinionator.blogs.nytimes.com.

62. Heffernan, "Miss G."

63. Quoted in Stephanie Pappas, "Today's Kids Face 'Facebook Depression,'" Live Science, March 28, 2011. www.livescience.com.

64. Quoted in CNET News, "Study Shows Some Suffer from 'Facebook Envy," February 3, 2011. http://news.cnet.com.

65. Quoted in Linda Shrieves, "Facebook May Help Identify Those with Depression, Study Says," *Orlando Sentinel*, March 28, 2011. http://articles.orlandosentinel.com.

66. Jenna Wortham, "Feel Like a Wallflower? Maybe It's Your Facebook Wall," *New York Times*, April 9, 2011. www.nytimes.com.

67. Mark Bauerlein, *The Dumbest Generation: How the Digital Age Stupefies Young Americans and Jeopardizes Our Future*. New York: Tarcher/Penguin, 2008, p. 26.

68. Don Tapscott, *Grown Up Digital: How the Net Generation Is Changing Your World*. New York: McGraw Hill, 2009, p. 2.

69. Tapscott, *Grown Up Digital*, p. 6.

70. Quoted in Rekindling the Reformation, "Elvis, Jerry Lee Lewis and Christianity." http://rekindlingthereformation.com.

71. Quoted in Baym, *Personal Connections in the Digital Age*, pp. 25–26.

Chapter Five: The Future of Online Social Media

72. Quoted in Kaku, *Physics of the Future*, p. 7.

73. YouTube, "1994: 'Today': 'What Is the Internet, Anyway?'" January 28, 2011. www.youtube.com.

74. Quoted in Jenna Wortham and Claire Cain Miller, "Social Networks Offer a Way to Narrow the Field of Friends," *New York Times*, May 9, 2001. www.nytimes.com.

75. Quoted in Wortham and Miller, "Social Networks Offer a Way to Narrow the Field of Friends."

76. Quoted in CBS News, "Conn. MBA Grads Start Social Site 'shizzlr.com,'" February 12, 2011. www.cbsnews.com.

77. Quoted in Wortham and Miller, "Social Networks Offer a Way to Narrow the Field of Friends."

78. Quoted in Jenna Wortham, "Focusing on the Social, Minus the Media," *New York Times*, June 4, 2011. www.nytimes.com.

79. Quoted in Eric Niiler, "Facebook Can Serve as Personality Test," Discovery News, May 9, 2011. http://news.discovery.com.

80. Quoted in Danny Westneat, "A Gr8 Kid's Tweets Not Exactly LOL," *Seattle Times*, May 7, 2001. http://seattletimes.nwsource.com.

81. Quoted in Sharon Gaudin, "U.S. Senator Urges FTC to Regulate Social Net Privacy," *Computerworld,* April 26, 2010. www.comput erworld.com.

82. Quoted in Lance Howland, "Wireless Technology to Make Parking Spaces 'Smart' in LA and SF," PublicCEO.com, March 25, 2010. http://publicceo.com.

83. Nicholas Carr, *The Big Switch: Rewiring the World, from Edison to Google.* New York: W.W. Norton, 2008, p. 81.

84. Kaku, *Physics of the Future,* p. 24.

85. Turkle, *Alone Together,* p. 285.

86. Janna Anderson and Lee Rainie, "The Future of Social Relations," Pew Internet and American Life Project, July 2, 2010. www.pewin ternet.org.

87. Quoted in Jemima Kiss, "Facebook Leaps into Future as Smart- phones Prepare to Get Smarter," *Guardian* (Manchester, UK), Janu- ary 16, 2011. www.guardian.co.uk.

Facts About Online Communication and Social Networking

- Yahoo! News reported that the April 2011 British royal wedding between Prince William and Kate Middleton was a Tweet-free zone. Cell phone–blocking technology was turned on early on the morning of the ceremony and remained in force until the nuptials were completed.

- Nearly 40 percent of Americans report that they have either been hit or nearly hit by drivers who have been using cell phones, according to a survey by Nationwide Insurance Company.

- In 2009 the US Department of Transportation reported that 995 deaths were directly attributable to use of cell phones while driving. While it is not known how many of them involved texting, the number is likely to be high.

- American teens send or receive an average of 3,339 texts a month, according to *School Library Journal*.

- In the United States, 77 percent of people between the ages of 18 and 29 use social networking, while just 23 percent of those 50 and over do so, says the Pew Research Center.

- Nearly half—48 percent—of young people between the ages of 12 and 17 say they have been a passenger in a car whose driver has been texting, according to the Pew Research Center.

- French television and radio cannot use "Facebook" and "Twitter" in news stories unless the usage refers to the companies themselves, the *New York Times* reports. That is because a 1992 law forbids the promotion of commercial enterprises on news programs.

- Twitter servers briefly crashed in 2009 after Michael Jackson's death, the BBC reports, because so many people were updating their status to include the pop singer's name.

- *Time* magazine says that users uploaded more video to YouTube in two months than were created by US TV networks NBC, ABC, and CBS in 60 years.

- The first e-mail was sent in 1969 between computers at Stanford University and the University of California at Los Angeles (UCLA), according to a report in London's *Daily Mail.*

- In May 2011 Twitter Counter reported that Lady Gaga had the most Twitter followers (10,338,665). She was followed by Justin Bieber (9,871,183) and President Barack Obama (8,184,675).

- As of August 2010, 41.6 percent of the US population had a Facebook account (128.9 million out of 309.9 million), said *Social Media Today.*

- The US Department of Transportation reports that at any given moment during daylight hours, more than 800,000 vehicles on American roads are being driven by someone holding a cell phone.

- As of March 2011, Yahoo! Mail and Windows Live Hotmail rank close together as the two most popular e-mail providers, with Google in third, according to e-mail Marketing Reports.

- There were more than 5 billion worldwide mobile phone connections by mid-July 2010, and experts predict the number will reach 6 billion by 2012, according to a report published by the UK's BBC News.

Related Organizations

American Library Association (ALA)

50 E. Huron St.
Chicago, IL 60611
phone: (800) 545-2433
fax: (312) 440-9374
e-mail: ala@ala.org
website: www.ala.org

The ALA is the professional association representing the nation's librarians. Visitors to the ALA website can find many resources about e-books and other Internet-based trends affecting American libraries. Several reports and updates on the ALA's program to encourage Library 2.0 initiatives in American libraries are also available.

Crimes Against Children Research Center

126 Horton Social Science Center
20 College Rd.
University of New Hampshire
Durham, NH 03824
phone: (603) 862-1888
e-mail: kelly.foster@unh.edu
website: www.unh.edu

The Crimes Against Children Research Center's primary mission is to provide reliable research to the general public, law enforcement organizations, and legislative bodies. It investigates a wide variety of child-related criminal activity, both on and off the Internet.

Facebook

1601 South California Ave.
Palo Alto, CA 94304
phone: (650) 543-4800
fax: (650) 543-4800
e-mail: info@facebook.com
website: www.facebook.com

Facebook is the world's largest social networking website. Members establish their own pages, which enable them to share comments, photos, and videos. In turn, they can access other members' pages. The company also provides messaging services among its users, as well as mobile applications for Java-powered feature phones.

Federal Communications Commission (FCC)

445 12th St. SW
Washington, DC 20554
phone: (888) 225-5322
fax: (866) 418-0232
e-mail: fccinfo@fcc.gov
website: www.fcc.gov

The Federal Communications Commission oversees regulations that affect electronic media in America, including the Internet. Students seeking information on net neutrality can find many resources on the agency's website, including statements in support of or opposition to net neutrality by the five FCC commissioners.

Google

1600 Amphitheatre Pkwy.
Mountain View, CA 94043
phone: (650) 253-0000
fax: (650) 253-0001
website: www.google.com

Students can find a lot of information about Google, the world's most popular search engine, by visiting the company's website. Students can learn about Google's history, its commitment to organizing the world's information, and the status of the company's many projects, including Google Books.

National Newspaper Association (NNA)

120A E. Broad St.
Falls Church, VA 22046-4501
phone: (800) 829-4662
fax: (703) 237-9808
website: www.nnaweb.org

The NNA represents the publishers of American newspapers. The organization has compiled many resources on how the Internet has affected American journalism. By entering "Internet" in the NNA website search engine, students can find more than 150 articles and reports that assess the value of online news.

Pew Internet & American Life Project

1615 L St. NW, Suite 700
Washington, DC 20036
phone: (202) 419-4500
fax: (202) 419-4505
e-mail: info@pewinternet.org
website: http://pewinternet.org

The Pew Internet & American Life Project studies how Americans use the Internet and how digital technologies are shaping the world today.

Twitter

795 Folsom St., Suite 600
San Francisco, CA 94107
website: www.twitter.com

Twitter is a social network that utilizes the principle of followers. In "Tweets" of a maximum of 140 characters, users can send messages to their followers and receive messages from those whom they are following. Twitter also has a "retweet" function, which allows original messages to be passed along to others.

YouTube

901 Cherry Ave.
San Bruno, CA 94066
phone: (650) 253-0000
fax: (650) 253-0001
website: www.youtube.com

YouTube is the world's largest video-sharing community. Students can find personalized recommendations based on their previous viewings. The site also includes daily features, the most popular videos in several categories, blogs, and more.

Wikimedia Foundation

149 New Montgomery St., 3rd Floor
San Francisco, CA 94105
phone: (415) 839-6885
fax: (415) 882-0495
e-mail: info@wikimedia.org
website: http://wikimediafoundation.org

Wikimedia Foundation is the nonprofit organization that administers the online encyclopedia Wikipedia. Visitors to the organization's website can find information on how Wikipedia is written as well as details on other projects, including the free online dictionary Wiktionary and a free source of e-books, Wikibooks.

For Further Research

Books

Mark Bauerlein, *The Dumbest Generation: How the Digital Age Stupefies Young Americans and Jeopardizes Our Future*. New York: Tarcher/Penguin, 2008.

Nancy Baym, *Personal Connections in the Digital Age*. Malden, MA: Polity, 2010.

Nicholas Carr, *The Big Switch: Rewiring the World, from Edison to Google*. New York: W.W. Norton, 2008.

———, *The Shallows: What the Internet Is Doing to Our Brains*. New York: W.W. Norton, 2010.

Edward Glaeser, *Triumph of the City: How Our Greatest Invention Makes Us Richer, Smarter, Greener, Healthier and Happier*. New York: Penguin, 2011.

Michio Kaku, *Physics of the Future: How Science Will Shape Human Destiny and Our Daily Lives by the Year 2100*. New York: Doubleday, 2011.

David Kirkpatrick, *The Facebook Effect: The Inside Story of the Company That Is Connecting the World*. New York: Simon & Schuster, 2010.

Ben Mezrich, *The Accidental Billionaires: The Founding of Facebook—a Tale of Sex, Money, Genius, and Betrayal*. New York: Doubleday, 2009.

Evgeny Morozov, *The Net Delusion: The Dark Side of Internet Freedom*. New York: PublicAffairs, 2011.

Don Tapscott, *Grown Up Digital: How the Net Generation Is Changing Your World*. New York: McGraw Hill, 2009.

Sherry Turkle, *Alone Together: Why We Expect More from Technology and Less from Each Other*. New York: Basic Books, 2011.

Siva Vaidhyanathan, *The Googlization of Everything (And Why We Should Worry)*. Berkeley and Los Angeles: University of California Press, 2011.

Periodicals

Aryn Baker, "How Can We Trust Them?," *Time*, May 20, 2011.

Sharon Begley, "I Can't Think!," *Newsweek*, March 7, 2011.

Mike Giglio, "The Facebook Freedom Fighter," *Newsweek*, February 21, 2011.

Malcolm Gladwell, "Small Change: Why the Revolution Will Not Be Tweeted," *New Yorker*, October 4, 2010.

Websites

Cybersafety: Protecting Your Kids and Teens Online (www.attorney general.gov/uploadedFiles/Consumers/cybersafety.pdf). A publication of the Pennsylvania attorney general but applicable everywhere; brochure format includes statistics, warning signs, tips on coping, and more.

Distraction.gov (www.distraction.gov/stats-and-facts). The official US government website about driving while distracted contains statistics, laws of various states, and research. One of the most important parts shows pictures of victims of distracted drivers and tells their stories.

Heather's Story (http://heathersstory.org). This is a website administered by Heather Lerch's parents to convey their anti-texting-while-driving message. Its resources include the story of Heather's life and other videos, photos, news relating to texting while driving, a continually updated Twitter feed, a blog, and more.

Mashable (http://mashable.com). Mashable is a website founded in 2005 to primarily cover social media news and offer web tips. With continuous updates and daily articles, Mashable is a gold mine of information for students doing reports on almost any aspect of Internet communication and social networking. The site also offers a calendar of upcoming events and sponsors the annual Mashable Awards (formerly known as Open Web Awards).

Microsoft Safety and Security Center (www.microsoft.com/security/default.aspx). This website is Microsoft's official online safety and security center. While it is geared for adults, teenagers will also find it useful. It contains information about protecting computers and personal information, recognizing scams, and building strong passwords to maintain Internet privacy. Visitors will also find security updates and free downloads.

NetSmartz Workshop (www.netsmartz.org/Parents). Netsmartz is the official website of the National Center for Missing and Exploited Children. Separate sections geared for teens, for tweens, and for children include advice on dealing with online predators, cyberbullying, misuse of cell phones, and similar issues. The site includes games, videos, and—for teens—a tipline to report potential abuses.

"A Parent's Guide to Internet Safety" (www.fbi.gov/stats-services/publications/parent-guide). An official FBI presentation offering signs of online risk, how to take action, and frequently asked questions.

SafeKids.com (www.safekids.com). Safe Kids is an offshoot of the California-based Tech Parenting Group and administered by technology journalist Larry Magid. It recently merged with Safe Teens and offers advice and Internet safety tools for children and teenagers. These include Google SafeSearch and tips on a wide variety of cybersubjects.

Safe Online Searching Internet Challenge (www.fbi-sos.org/index.cfm?Page=Students). The Safe Online Searching Internet Challenge is an FBI-affiliated quiz program on Internet safety for grades 3 through 8. Schools scoring the highest receive a trophy and visit from FBI agents.

"We Are All Khalid Said" (www.facebook.com/elshaheeed.co.uk). This is Khalid Said's Facebook page and has ongoing coverage of developments in Egypt and elsewhere. The page also has background information about Khalid and photos of him before and after his beating (warning: the latter are very graphic).

Index

Note: Boldface page numbers indicate illustrations.

Picture Credits

Cover: Thinkstock/Photodisc
Maury Aaseng: 14
AP Images: 5, 9, 19, 25, 29, 33, 37, 41, 45, 62, 67, 73
© Arthur Klonsky/Corbis: 49
Thinkstock/BananaStock: 53
Thinkstock/iStockphoto: 60

About the Author

Jim Whiting has published more than 100 nonfiction books for young readers and has also edited nearly 200 titles. His diverse writing career includes 17 years as publisher of *Northwest Runner* magazine, advising a national award-winning high school newspaper, writing and photography for America Online, serving as sports editor for the *Bainbridge Island Review*, and hundreds of articles for newspapers and magazines.